A Prescrip ... .

The Love Doctor:

How to find Love in 7 Easy Steps

A Prescription from
The Love Doctor:
How to find Love in 7 Easy Steps

Joanne Coyle, Ph.D.

First edition
Published in Great Britain
By Mirage Publishing 2008

Text Copyright © Dr Joanne Coyle 2008

First published in paperback 2008

A CIP catalogue record for this book
Is available from the British Library.

ISBN: 978-1-90257-836-1

Mirage Publishing
PO Box 161
Gateshead
NE8 4WW
Great Britain

Printed and bound in Great Britain by

Book Printing UK
Remus House, Coltsfoot Drive, Woodston, Peterborough, PE2 9JX

Cover © Mirage Publishing

Layout by Book Printing UK

Papers used in the production of this book are recycled,
thus reducing environmental depletion.

To Mum, Jan and Amy for all things past, present and future, and particularly to Dave my lover and friend.

Contents

Introduction

You hold in your hands a book that has the power to change your love life forever. It is your magical guide for your journey to a happy, loving, and committed relationship. This book contains powerful psychological spells and tools that will equip you on this journey, should you choose to take it, and will ensure that you have the best possible chance of reaching your desired destination. Don't underestimate the power of the techniques in this book. They might just change your life!

People in happy, loving, successful relationships aren't simply lucky. They have created this happy situation for themselves by acting and thinking in certain ways that I'll now be sharing with you.

My Journey

How can I be so sure that you'll attain the relationship of your dreams simply by reading this book? My evidence is my own amazing experience and that of my clients.

Let me tell you about my journey. I had a satisfying career as a university lecturer and researcher. My income was steadily rising. I had my own home. I enjoyed holidays abroad. I had an active social life, attending various leisure classes and participating in salsa dancing, jazz dancing and yoga in my spare time. Not a bad life, eh?

I wasn't complaining. I was successful in all areas of my life - except one. At forty-two, I hadn't been romantically involved with a man for a number of years. Despite my active social life, I longed for a secure, loving relationship, yet I had a vague feeling that something was holding me back. In many of my past relationships I had felt emotionally insecure. I sensed a self-defeating pattern.

I felt as if I'd read every book available on love, relationships, personal development and 'mind, body, spirit'. Although these books had taught me a lot about myself and I'd found many of these works deeply interesting, they hadn't brought me any closer to the relationship I longed for.

Then I came across a set of magical tools called Neuro-Linguistic Programming (NLP) and a wonderful shamanism called Huna from the Hawaiian Islands. NLP and Huna contain an astonishingly simple yet highly effective set of almost magical psychological techniques that help people to change their lives by changing how they think and feel. I wanted to tackle the one area that success had eluded me: relationships. So I enrolled in a number of NLP courses. I became first a practitioner and then a master practitioner of NLP, Time-Line Therapy and hypnotherapy, and ultimately an NLP coach. I now help people from all walks of life in achieving their most highly valued goals and dreams, especially in relationships.

I learned that truly magical practitioners of NLP study people who are highly successful in a particular area of their lives and then discern exactly how these people have achieved their success. This process provides a model of techniques, strategies and thought patterns (spells if you will) that others can copy to succeed in their own lives. This method has been phenomenally successful in business, sales, marketing and therapy and now I believe can do the same for those searching for love.

The shamanic practices in Huna enable individuals to let go of negative emotions, troubling past relationships, and beliefs, which may be holding them back from getting the kind of loving relationship they long for.

Taking everything I had learned in these courses and drawing on my fifteen years' experience researching human behaviour, I adapted these tools and techniques specifically to love and relationships. I began by applying this newly refined system to my own situation and was astounded to find myself in a loving, committed, supportive and passionate relationship within only ten months! That was four years ago. After all these years, I am now

Introduction

in a loving, committed relationship with a man who loves me and cares for me and whom I love and care for. What a result! Since that time I have helped many others to achieve similar success.

I can find no higher or stronger endorsement of the bewitching system in this book than my own experience. It literally changed my life and the lives of my clients. And I believe it will change your life too.

You Too Can Find Love

Maybe you're reading this book because you're struggling (as I was) to enjoy being single. Maybe you feel that something is missing in your life, or you've noticed recurring patterns in your relationships that you want to eliminate. Maybe it's been some time since your last relationship, or maybe your current relationship isn't working. Maybe you feel, as I did, that something is holding you back from achieving what you really want in life: that loving, committed relationship.

Whatever the reason for you not being in a loving relationship yet, I would say this to you: I believe that we are all capable of creating and sustaining committed, loving relationships. There's nothing like the feeling of being loved, cared for and passionately desired by another human being. And there's nothing like loving, caring for and passionately desiring another person. I believe that being physically and emotionally close to another person satisfies a basic, deep-seated human need - through their touch, the way they hold us, the way they look at us, through their words and the tone of their voice.

I am now convinced that that each and every one of us has a deep desire to be intimately and lovingly connected with another human being. It is part of our make-up, almost part of our DNA. It's what drives us to get out of bed in the morning and keeps us going when things get tough. It has even been known to drive us to distraction. Psychologists Diener and Seligman conducted research among extremely happy people and found that every person apart from one in the top ten per cent of the most happy

Dr Joanne 'The Love Doctor' Coyle

people were either married or in a long-term committed relationship. Marriage and long-term commitment is now recognised to be the most powerful factor to happiness, over and above job satisfaction, finances and the community.

Many of us have not yet achieved this desire because of our own negative beliefs and unresolved emotions. In this book I'll show you how to deal with such beliefs and feelings easily and comfortably. If you really want to have the relationship you dream about, I urge you to follow the instructions and diligently practice the techniques. Chances are you'll find what you've been looking for.

Your journey will take you through a number of stages. Make sure you allow yourself sufficient time to work through this book at your own pace and without distractions. Dedicate fifteen minutes or half an hour each day to absorbing and practicing some small but powerful technique. Practical exercises throughout the book will help you stay on track.

This book guides you through seven levels of profound transformation in your consciousness, leading you to the ultimate level of awareness where you will know with absolute certainty that the relationship you desire has arrived. This may happen before you finish the book, when you get to the end of the book or shortly after completing all the tasks in the book. The first seven levels end with simple actions for you to take before for you to proceed to the next level. You will have fun and make startling discoveries about yourself as you do this. Be amazed as your life begins to change and new opportunities appear all around you. Be sure to look out for those opportunities!

Level 1 helps you to understand how you've created your current situation and what you need to do to create the kind of love life you want. You'll learn to use the startling magic of your unconscious mind, to bring a loving relationship into your life.

At Level 2 you'll discover what you most want from a relationship. Be warned this may be different from what you think your want! You'll learn what you value most in life and love and what drives you. You'll discover your purpose in life and why

xii

this is essential to securing the type of love life you truly desire. You'll also learn how to set relationship goals that will actually come true.

At Level 3 you'll understand how to control your emotions so that you achieve emotional freedom. You'll learn the secret of how to choose your emotional state. You'll be given the tools and spells to create the best, most productive, feelings in any situation. You'll understand how emotional freedom can help you to create a happy, successful relationship.

As you proceed to Level 4 you'll discover the secret of charisma. You'll find out what makes a person attractive to others and how the words and actions of charismatic people make them appealing. You'll learn how to get on with everyone you meet and how to be a people magnet. You'll know how to have greater influence in any of your relationships. By the time you've reached the end of this Level you'll have learned how to develop trusting, supportive relationships.

At Level 5 you'll find out about the astounding magic of beliefs. You'll understand how your beliefs have determined your life so far, and how changing your beliefs about yourself, other people and relationships can change your life forever. You'll learn an easy way to identify the beliefs that are holding you back from finding the relationship you want. Finally, you'll be given the tools to transform self-defeating beliefs into empowering ones that will help get you into your dream relationship.

Level 6 will help you to understand how the mind affects the body and what you can do to maximise your health and well-being. You'll be given tips and strategies to increase your energy levels, self-confidence and to achieve your ideal weight and body shape. You will feel more attractive and confident than you've ever felt before. You'll also be given tools that you can use anywhere to relax and calm yourself.

Level 7 will help you understand why your love life is the way it is. You'll understand the choices you've made in your relationships: why you chose a particular person, why a particular person chose you, why your relationships follow a particular pattern or why you haven't had a relationship for a while. You'll learn how the experiences and relationships you were exposed to in childhood come to be replicated in adulthood. You'll also discover how to overcome any problem patterns from your past. As we go through this Level, I'll share the most powerful and magical techniques I know to get at the root cause of the problems you've been experiencing in relationships and dissolve the emotions associated with them.

At the final Level you will be shown how to create your future exactly the way you want it. You'll learn how to apply love magic to your future so that the goals you set and the dreams you hold dear actually come true. Like many others who have mastered these techniques, you can become one of those 'lucky' people who are amazingly successful in love. What would that be like?

Stop for a moment and imagine this scenario: What would it be like if you woke up one morning and found that you had the relationship of your dreams? Imagine it vividly; really be there in your body, looking out through your eyes.

How do you know that you have the relationship of your dreams? What do you see? What do you hear? How do you feel?

What if you read this book and practice all the skills you've learned? Suppose that any self-limiting beliefs you may have had are eliminated. Imagine that you know how to heal your emotions and you know how to program your future, so that the relationship goals you set actually do happen. What will you go for? How much happier and more fulfilled will you be? What would you expect of a relationship? What sort of fantastic relationship will you now have? Only you can know.

How to Use This Book

I sincerely hope you've chosen to embark on this journey. If so, this magical guide will show you exactly how to achieve your successful relationship. The spells and techniques in this book can transform your love life if you're willing to take the time and effort to follow the instructions for materialising love precisely.

Introduction

I'm confident that if you commit to working through all the processes in this book, you can make your dreams come true. So give yourself some space and quality time to get to where you want to be. You're worth it.

Enjoy the journey.

Level 1

Know What You Have to Do –
Use the Magic of your Unconscious Mind

"We all want to love and be loved, and yet finding love and keeping it alive can seem to be the greatest challenge we face." Ariana Gee and Mary Gregory, *Be Your Own Love* Coach (P10 2005).

Let me begin by asking you some questions. The answers you give will determine whether you'll find what you're looking for. If someone offered to act as your mentor and guide you to finding and keeping the loving, committed relationship you long for, would you accept the offer? Would you follow their guidance? Would you do what is asked of you? Would you listen and follow instructions? If I showed you where to look for the relationship of your dreams, would you look there? Would you go there? Would you be willing to look at yourself and change yourself?

Let me begin by telling you a story. This story was told to me by a friend. He heard it from his granddad, who had learned it from his father many years before. It was about a man who was travelling on board a steam train, way back in the early 1900s. The train had stopped in the darkness and the man pushed down the window to see what had happened. He rested his elbows on the window frame, and looked this way and that to find out the cause of the delay. Being unable to see anything, he turned around and sat down. Then he noticed his house keys were missing. He began to frantically search around the carriage, and soon many of his fellow passengers joined him in his search until one finally asked, 'Where exactly did you lose your keys?' The man replied 'Outside, when I leaned out of the window'.

Astonished, the passenger asked, 'Then why are you looking in here?'

The man said, 'Because it's lighter in here'.

The moral of this tale is if you spend your life searching for answers outside yourself, you cannot possibly find the answers to change your life. Nobody knows you better than you know yourself. Once you begin to look within, the answers come intuitively, and you'll find that the solutions to the challenges you face in life will come to you more easily and more often.

Now that I know you are willing to examine yourself and make the effort to change yourself, we can begin. You have already taken the first step towards achieving the relationship you desire.

If you're reading this book, you've probably thought about the problem a great deal. Perhaps you've tried to understand the reasons why you are not yet in a loving and supportive relationship, or why there have been destructive patterns in your previous relationships. Maybe, like me, you've read a great many self-help books. Yet, even though you've thought about the problem a lot, you haven't been able to solve it yet, have you? If you had, you wouldn't be reading this book.

When you think about a problem and try to analyse it, you are using your conscious mind. The first thing you need to understand is that the problem is NOT in the conscious, rational part of your mind. If it was, then it stands to reason that you would have solved it by now. Understand that any change, any progress you make in love, will come from working with your amazing *unconscious* mind. It is only by communicating with your unconscious mind (and thereby connecting with your Higher Self) can you make profound lasting changes in your life.

Use the Magical Power of Your Unconscious Mind to Bring Love into Your Life

To use your unconscious mind effectively, you need to understand what it is and how it works. Let's begin by contrasting it with the conscious mind. Simply, the conscious mind refers to everything we're currently aware of, what we're focusing on, what we're thinking of *now*. Research has shown that we are consciously aware of only around seven pieces of information at any given time. Yet, as you sit reading this book, your eyes are taking in information from around the room, the light, the colours and the shapes. Your ears are picking up the frequency, tone and timbre of the slightest sounds. You're also feeling through your skin the touch of fabric, the hardness or softness of your chair; maybe you're feeling hungry or thirsty. You may also be picking up certain smells or tastes. You are being bombarded with information from all directions from one second to the next. Over your lifetime billions of pieces of information enter your nervous system.

What happens to all of that information? It enters the unconscious mind that contains everything - all the thoughts, feelings, sensations, beliefs and values - that you aren't paying attention to at this moment. It's the repository of all your memories, of everything that you've ever experienced. It stores your memories according to a time sequence so you know that one thing happened before another. It also stores memories according to a particular subject or theme. So, you may hold a collection of memories about feeling happy and another collection about feeling sad or betrayed.

Your mind is like a huge iceberg. An iceberg sits in the water and only a small part of it is visible above the surface, while underneath there is a huge mass. The portion above the surface represents the conscious mind, while the unconscious mind, by far biggest and most powerful part, remains unseen below the surface. The unconscious part contains all awareness and information that the conscious mind is not currently focussed on. All memories, feelings and thoughts that we are not consciously aware of are by definition 'unconscious'.

You can see now, that your unconscious mind is more knowing and powerful than the conscious mind. It remembers everything that has happened in our lives; it is the storehouse and the origin of our emotions; and it is the part of us that has a direct connection with our Spirit or Higher Self and with each other.

Many of your values, beliefs and feelings will remain unconscious without your ever knowing how powerful they are in guiding your life. If you want to deal with any troubling emotions about love and relationships then you must go to your unconscious mind. We now have simple and effective psychological tools that can help you resolve many negative emotions and conflicts at the Level of your unconscious mind.

Troubling emotions are like messages being delivered to your front door. If you don't answer, it keeps knocking, if you still don't answer it knocks louder, if you still don't answer then it knocks even louder and keeps knocking until you finally open the door. It then delivers you the message. As soon as you understand the message and you learn something about yourself, you become emotionally stronger. This is an important part of emotional healing. Here's a simple way to understand the true message that lies underneath any bad feeling.

Discovering the Hidden Message

1. Focus on the troubling feeling. Do not think about what caused it or what happened, just let yourself feel the emotion itself. Be aware of where in the body you feel it and really connect with the emotion. Is it in your stomach, your chest, or your head? Does it have a shape? If it had a colour, what colour would it be? Is it moving at all?

2. Now ask yourself what the feeling is about. Allow the answer to just pop into your mind. You might get another feeling, or you may see an image, or a word or memory may pop into your head.

3. If another feeling arises ask what that feeling is about. If another comes up ask what that feeling is about. Keep going until you come to the feeling that is underneath all these other feelings. Usually, you will discover a feeling you have about yourself.

4. Now ask yourself what is the purpose of this underlying feeling? Ask what its intention is? Keep asking its' purpose until you come to an answer or intention that is positive. That is, the intention of the feeling is that it wants something good for you.

This is very important.

5. Focus on the good intention. Ask yourself if there are any other ways of satisfying this good intention. For example, if the highest positive intention was 'to make you feel happy', you would ask yourself if there are any things you could do now to make you feel happy. You might decide to visit friends, organise a party or join a gym! Now that you understand more about yourself, you no longer need the bad feeling. You have received and understood the message.

Use the Untapped Potential of the Unconscious Mind to Bring Love into Your Life

The unconscious mind has huge untapped potential that can enable you to get what you most want in life and love. The human brain has ten to fifteen billion neurons and connections. In addition, it has a supportive system of fifty to eighty billion neuralgia cells that act as backups to the neurons. Yet, scientists have found that we use only around ten percent of the available neuron connections. That ten percent is the conscious mind. With 90 percent of your mind left dormant and unguided, it's little wonder if you haven't yet achieved your ideal relationship. The latent potential power of your unconscious mind to get you what you desire in life is now widely recognised.

Lets' think about our iceberg mind once more. Just below the tip of the iceberg is a tremendous latent power which is constantly taking action. Our conscious mind is continuously supported by unconscious resources in everything we do, even if we are unaware of it. Stop for a minute and think of all the things you know how to do without consciously thinking about them. If you drive, you use over thirty specific skills, yet scarcely being aware of any of them. At first, you had to consciously learn to drive, it required concentration, effort, intelligence, training and the ability to make decisions, but now many of your skills are unconscious. Although you had to think and concentrate at first, driving for many of you now is second nature.

Through the specific procedures and techniques in this book, which are almost like magic, you can now tap into that enormous reservoir of untapped capabilities and resources. As you begin to use your mind to its fullest potential, the chances of getting what you want will increase ten times and will be a lot easier than you imagine.

Telling Your Unconscious Mind What You Want

The second thing you need to know is how to give your unconscious mind instructions. Although your unconscious mind is responsible for the overwhelming majority of your mental and physiological functioning in some respects, it acts in ways very similar to a six year old child. Like a six-year-old child, it takes the things you say quite literally. For this reason, you have to be precise about what you ask it to do.

Often you don't give your unconscious mind any instructions at all, or at best confusing directions, so it's not surprising that it sometimes makes mistakes and creates situations and relationships that appear harmful and hurtful. However, since your unconscious mind is programmed by nature to act in your best interest, it's essential to give it precise instructions about what you want.

Many of my clients tell me what they don't want rather than what they do want. For example, they'll say, 'I don't want to feel insecure in a relationship' or 'I don't want to feel unhappy'. The problem is that the unconscious mind doesn't recognise negatives like *don't, not, doesn't* and *mustn't*, so it skips over the *don't wants* and *must nots* and focuses on the rest of the sentence. If you gave it the first example as an instruction - 'I don't want to feel insecure in a relationship' - what would your unconscious mind focus on? That's right, the part of the sentence that talks about feeling *insecure* in a relationship. When you give instructions to your unconscious mind you must make sure they are precise and stated positively: for example, 'I want to feel secure in a loving, committed relationship'.

The only reason why people do not have what they want is because they are thinking more about what they *don't* want than what they *do* want. Listen to your thoughts, and listen to the words you are saying. The law is absolute and there are no limits.

Have you ever thought about something that was bothering you, and the more you thought about it the worse it seemed? That's because if you focus your attention on one thought for long enough, the law of attraction will immediately bring other similar thoughts to you. In a matter of minutes, so many similar worrying thoughts will be 'popping' into your head that the situation will appear to be getting worse. The more you think about the issue, the more upset you get.

Your unconscious mind will take many things you think and say as instructions or suggestions, whether you intend it to or not. This situation is fine when you're thinking optimistically and generously about others and yourself but not so good if you're being critical. Say you see someone at the gym or fitness class and you think, 'Wow. She looks fantastic. What a great body. I'll bet she's really fit and healthy. I'll bet she really enjoys life. I want a body like hers. I want to be fit and healthy and look like that'. Your unconscious mind takes your thoughts as a suggestion and works towards creating such a situation for you because it believes that's what you want. If, on the other hand, you think less charitably and more enviously, 'Huh! It's not fair that she has a body like that. Bet she doesn't have any fun. She must really control her diet and work out at the gym twelve hours a day', then your unconscious mind will take this description as what you want and create a situation that you can have the body you desire only if you eat very little, have no fun and spend many hours at the gym.

Since your unconscious mind takes everything you *say* (as well as think) as a suggestion, any unkind words or thoughts about another person will affect you personally. If you say to your friend, 'so and so doesn't deserve a relationship like that', your unconscious mind will attempt to create a situation in which you feel that you don't deserve your own relationship.

So be careful what you think, what you wish for and what you say. Think of your thoughts and words about others and yourself as food that can either nourish your body and mind or undermine them. If you see someone who has something you'd like for yourself, someone who is living the lifestyle you want, or someone who is being the kind of person you'd love to be, think uplifting thoughts about that person. Think how great life is for her or him. Wish them happiness and luck, and let your unconscious mind create the same happiness and luck for you. Your unconscious mind is a servant and will always try to get you what you want.

Filling your mind with positive thoughts about others and yourself, will change the image you have of yourself. You will come to see yourself as a kinder and more positive person. This new self-image will attract a new and more vibrant energy into your love life, and your life in general. In the same way as positive thoughts help you reach you love goals, so do the images that you hold in your head. Whatever you constantly see, hear or feel about your future in your mind, will eventually come true for you in some way.

So let's stop for a moment to focus on what you really want. Let's instil a positive movie for you to run again and again about your love life. You will attract love into your life simply by focusing on your ideal relationship.

Your Dream Lover

1. Close your eyes. Imagine that you are looking at your dream partner. How is he behaving? What is he saying? What is he doing? How is he looking at you?
2. Now see you and him together. Where are you? What are you doing? How are you behaving toward each other? Notice how loving, caring and supportive he is.
3. Now feel what it would be like to be totally loved, appreciated and desired. Really feel those great feelings. Know what it is like to be so loved and desired by your man.

4. See both of you together and know that your partner is honest, dependable, trustworthy, loyal and respectful.

The Three Pillars of Success

Now that you understand more about your unconscious mind, how can you get it to work best for you? What can you do to ensure that, consciously and unconsciously, you're creating the life and the relationship you want? To achieve what you most desire in a relationship you must accept these three powerful ideas.

Firstly, you are the *creator* of *everything* in your world. That is, you are in some way responsible (consciously or, more often, unconsciously) for all that you've experienced. Now, before you jump up and down in exasperation, let me clarify what I mean by this statement. I don't mean that you're to blame for all the things, good and bad, that have ever happened to you. This is not about blame or about fault. So get that thought out of your mind. I mean that in nearly every situation your unconscious mind has created what it *thought* you wanted.

Remember, I said that your unconscious mind is like a six-year-old child. If you don't give it clear, precise instructions a six year old child will inevitably makes mistakes. It may seem hard at first to accept that you've somehow created everything in your life, especially if you're facing challenges. But stop and think for a moment. If you've created a life you don't want, you *must* also have the power to create the life you *do* want. All you need to know is how to use this power. Accepting that you're responsible for your life is actually a step towards regaining power over your life.

Second, everything around you - people, relationships, events and circumstances - is a *projection* of what's *inside of you*. Problems with certain people or certain relationships happen because you have a problem or conflict deep within yourself. In other words, what you perceive in the world around you is a projection of your own inner world. During the rest of the day notice what's going on, what's happening around you. Reflect on what you're projecting onto the world. Some of it is likely to be good. Maybe you feel emotionally supported by your friends, or you felt appreciated at work today. Other things may not be so good. Maybe you had an argument with a colleague or you feel that your family takes you for granted.

The wonderful thing is that you can change your relationships and your circumstances by changing your inner world, and what you project. You can change your inner world by resolving any internal conflicts and eliminating doubts you unconsciously hold. As you go through the following Levels in this book, I will show you simple techniques or spells to help you resolve these conflicts and embark on your journey of transformation and personal development.

Finally, *you* must take one hundred percent *responsibility* for achieving your aspirations and dreams. Think for a moment about the relationship between an athlete and a coach. The coach will work with the athlete, offering advice, giving the athlete skills to practice, helping the athlete to change his or her thinking, but it's the athlete who applies the skills, who practices and who wins the race. It's the athlete who stands on the podium, the athlete who gets the gold medal and the praise because the athlete is ultimately one hundred percent responsible for achieving his or her goals. You are the athlete, it is your life and your relationship.

As your teacher I have one hundred percent confidence in the magic and the techniques in this book. I also have one hundred percent confidence in your ability to achieve your desired relationship using these techniques. I know it can be done because I have achieved a wonderful loving relationship and I've seen my clients achieve their dream relationships. No doubt you too know people who are involved in loving, committed relationships and marriages, so you know that it's possible. You already know that such people have created this happy situation for themselves by thinking, feeling and acting in certain ways. You too can achieve the same kinds of results by changing the way you think, feel and act.

So how can you change how you think and how your feel? Fortunately, Neuro-Linguistic Programming (NLP) and Huna, the ancient Hawaiian system of psychological magic, gives you simple, effective psychological tools to do just that. It's up to you to practice the techniques I'm about to share with you. Remember, only you can achieve your results. You're one hundred percent responsible for your success and YOU CAN DO IT.

Guiding Your Unconscious Mind to the Relationship of Your Dreams

As we come to the end of Lesson 1 it should be obvious that this book is essentially a magical guide for the unconscious mind. If it were possible for your conscious mind to achieve your dreams, you would have achieved them long ago because you've thought about them often enough. Right? You know consciously that you want a loving relationship and but you have not yet achieved it, so you must now go to your unconscious mind with precise instructions and guide it to overcome obstacles that have been holding you back. As you progress through the Levels simply notice how your life changes and how much happier you feel. Only you can discover the enormous difference that the magic in this book will make in your life.

Your Practical Magic for Level 1

1. *Perception is projection!* Be aware that everything around you is a projection of what's within. Notice all the good things and all the not so good. Make a mental note of what you're grateful for and what you can change within to make your life even better.
2. *Make positive statements!* Starting today, state everything you want in positive terms (no more 'I don't want this' or 'I can't do this'). Instead, use positive statements: 'I can understand this', 'this is easy', 'I can feel secure' and so on. Instead of focusing on

problems, focus on finding solutions.

3. *Make positive suggestions!* Be aware of all the suggestions you're giving to your unconscious mind when you think about other people. Starting today, look and listen for what's good and valuable in others.

You are now ready to move on to Level 2

Level 2

Know Where You Want to Go –
Spells for a Love Destination

Throughout our lives we travel to many destinations. Perhaps at some time we've decided that it's been a long winter and we'd like to go somewhere warm to relax and enjoy ourselves. Some of us have considered going to a beach resort on the Mediterranean, the Caribbean or the Pacific. The adventurous among us have wanted to go trekking in distant places, off the beaten track. Others have decided on somewhere closer to home.

When you went on holiday, you planned your route, organised transfers and timed your journey. But before that, you needed to decide on where you wanted to go: your holiday destination. It is obvious that if you want to reach your dream destination, or indeed any destination, you must first know where you want to go.

The spell of setting a goal for a relationship is just like deciding on a destination for a journey. If you don't have a goal for your relationship you won't go anywhere, or you'll lose a lot of time going up and down blind alleys and coming to dead ends (and dead end relationships). Here's the crucial thing. The main reason people don't get everything they want in their lives, including a successful relationship, is that they don't have goals. If you have a destination (goal) you're significantly more likely to reach your destination than if you don't know where you want to go. Goals give your life direction. A goal gives your unconscious mind clear, specific instructions about what you want and what it needs to work on to make your dream a reality.

Deciding Where You Want to Go - Your Love Goal

What exactly is a goal? A goal is a result that you want to create or a wonderful destination that you want to reach. You must be clear about your goal in order for it to come about. Goals are specific, not vague. For example, wanting to be happy is vague because it is a feeling you can have anytime if you choose. In fact, I will show you how to generate feelings of happiness anytime you want in Level 3! Goals are a specific end point, for example to be in a loving, committed relationship or be married. Goals involve taking action. You must take steps to get where you want to go.

Finally, goals are measurable—you can measure how far you need to go to reach your goal. For example, you may have an active social life and be meeting lots of men, you may be dating or you may not yet have widened your social circle. If you don't set a clear relationship goal and you are not certain about what you want, then you will drift aimlessly and never achieve a fulfilling relationship. You can't reach your love destination if you don't know where it is! Relationship experts stress that the most important step to gaining the relationship you want is to determine exactly what it is you want.

You should have a clear idea of the qualities and characteristics you are looking for in your dream lover. For many people love and attraction are a complete mystery. They don't know why they are drawn towards certain people. They remain unaware that they are always attracted to people with particular traits and qualities. They've never stopped to think about or understand why they became besotted in the first place. They are just like ships that are lost at sea without a compass or map to guide them. They seem to drift aimlessly with little control over their own destiny. But you can be different. If you understand the forces that guide you and know where you want to go, you can chart your own course and get to where you want to be. And that is what you are going to do.

When you choose your destination you'll become aware of the difference between where you are now and where you want to be. Setting a goal and being clear about what you want means you can plan your journey from here to there. It means you're on the road to achieving your goal. It's just like when you book your holiday, you already feel that you're on the way and you know with certainty that you'll get there. Joseph O'Connor, author of *The NLP Workbook*, says that personal change is a journey from an unsatisfactory present state of affairs towards your desired state, which is your result. When you don't know what you want you can be easily distracted by other people, who may divert you towards their desired results. For this reason, it's important to set your own goals.

The first step to casting a spell for achieving the relationship you want is to think your goals through clearly. What is it that you want? Why do you want it? Should you want it? Should you want something different? To achieve your relationship goals you must make sure they're realistic, motivating and can be achieved. How?

To embark on your journey into the relationship you desire, ask yourself the following four key questions:

- What am I moving towards? (The desired result)
- Why am I moving towards it? (What drives me?)
- How will I get there? (What plans and strategies do I have?)
- What if I encounter problems or obstacles? (How will I deal with them?)

Your answers will help you understand what you want, what drives and motivates you, how you can plan your journey to achieve your goal and what you can do should any obstacles present themselves.

Casting the Spell - How to Set a Relationship Goal so That You Actually Get There!

Now that you know why having goals is so crucial to achieving the kind of relationship you want, you need to know how to set goals to make them happen. To set love goals that drive you towards achieving them quickly, you must decide goals that satisfy certain well-established criteria, known in the business world as SMART. These goals must be:

S: Specific/Simple. Your goal must be simple, clear and unambiguous. You must state exactly what you want and how you want it.

M: Measurable/Meaningful. Your goal must be measurable. You must have clear criteria for success, so that you'll know when you've achieved it. For example, I'll know when I've achieved my love goal when I am walking arm and arm along a beach on holiday with my partner, or when we are standing at the alter saying 'I do'. It's up to you, but your goal must be meaningful to you. The goal must be what *you* desire and not what you think you *should* want or what other people want for you. It must be instigated by you and for you.

A: 'As if now'/Achievable. You must express your goal as if you already have it. For this reason, goals must be stated in the present tense, not the future tense, for example, a SMART goal would be phrased 'I am involved in a loving, committed relationship' rather than 'I *will* have a loving, committed relationship'. If you say 'I will be married' or 'I will be in a loving relationship', then the result to your unconscious will always be in the future. You will always be striving for something that stays in the future. So say your goal as if it has already happened. Say 'I'm loved'. 'I'm in a loving committed relationship'.

You must also 'act as if' you've already achieved your goal. Imagine you're in a wonderful relationship, the kind of relationship you really want, and 'act as if' it's true. How do you feel? How do you look? How do you act? What do you hear?

Your goals must also be achievable. For example, wanting to have a relationship with an international superstar like Brad Pitt who is already involved in a celebrity relationship doesn't seem imminently achievable! Having said that, remember it's also about what *you* think is achievable. For example, if you want a relationship with someone overseas, don't listen to other people's doubts about whether a loving, committed, long-distance relationship can be achievable. So long as you believe it, then go for it one hundred percent and you can achieve it.

'Acting as if' is a deceptively simple tip for instilling new, life-changing beliefs. It is simply to 'act as if' the belief were true. Astoundingly, 'acting as if' something is true makes it true. Of course, you don't have to take my word for it. Test it yourself.

'Acting as if' is a simple but effective method. Decide on what you *want* to believe and then 'act as if' it's true. Act as if you are receiving what your desire right now. Do exactly as you would do if you were in that wonderful relationship today. How would you be feeling? How would you be walking? How would you be interacting with people? Make your actions from now on reflect that powerful expectation. Make room in your life to receive a relationship, and as you do, you are sending out that powerful signal of expectation to the universe.

You don't have to actually believe it's true yet. For example, at the beginning of my relationship I 'acted as if' I was in a caring, committed and exciting relationship. Of course, it was too early to know whether that would be the case, but I observed the results I was getting by 'acting as if' this belief was true. Gradually, my 'reality' (my relationship) came to fit the belief and now I no longer have to 'act as if' I'm in a caring, committed and exciting relationship. If you like the results you get when you 'act as if', continue to 'act as if' they are true.

You can choose what you want to believe. If beliefs don't bring good results, change them. 'Act as if' something else.

R: Realistic/Ecological. Is your goal realistic? Are you one hundred percent sure that the goal can be achieved? For instance, have other people achieved the goal? Do you know other people who are happily married or in a loving committed relationship? If you do then you know the goal is possible and achievable. The next critical thing is…Do you believe that YOU CAN achieve the goal too? Some of you might think 'yeah, of course I can!' Great! Good for you. Others of you might not be so sure. Before my relationship materialised, because of my past failures in love, I did not believe that I could have a loving, committed, supportive long term relationship. So if you're like me, don't worry. All the techniques in this book are designed to increase your confidence and help you feel much more positive about achieving the relationship of your dreams.

Your love goal must also be ecological. That is, getting your goal must not harm you or any other person, or any other areas of your life. For example, wanting a relationship with a specific person who didn't want a relationship with you would not be ecological. Both parties must want the relationship. However, if you were attracted to someone but couldn't have a relationship with that person, you could set a responsible goal to have a relationship with someone with similar qualities. The goal you set must not harm any other areas of your life, such as your relationship with your family, your work, career, personal and spiritual development. Ideally it should enhance all areas of your life. Your ultimate aim should be to have a happy and balanced life, spending equal time on your career, relationship, personal and spiritual development, family and relaxation. Moreover, you should enjoy the time you spend in all areas of your life.

T: You must put your goal on a time scale. You should have a precise date by which you want your goal to be achieved, that is, the day, month and year. This date gives your unconscious mind precise instructions about when you want your goal, and it will work towards achieving it at that exact time.

The Keys to Achieving Your Goals

Now you know the criteria or conditions that your goals must meet. Next, you need to know how to set SMART relationship goals. Using the following nine questions will help you set realistic, ecological and achievable goals. Please read through all the questions first then proceed to the practical love goal materialisation exercise that follows.

1. *What specifically do you want?*

State your goal in positive terms. Goals should be directed *towards* something you want rather than *away from* something you want to avoid. Ask yourself, 'What do I want? What do I really want? What, specifically, do I want?' rather than 'What don't I want? What do I want to avoid?' For example, the statement 'I don't want to be alone' is a negative goal directed away from 'being alone'. Remember, the unconscious mind can't process a negative, so what does it focus on? Yes, that's right: 'being alone', and that is precisely what it will work on for you.

How do you turn a negative goal into a positive goal? Simply by asking, 'What do I want instead?' If you don't want to be alone, set a goal to become involved in a loving, supportive relationship.

2. *Where are you now?*

Describe where you are now in relation to your goal. What do you want to change? What isn't working for you?

3. *How will you know when you've achieved your goal?*
Imagine that you've achieved your goal. Picture the scene. What will you see? What will you hear? What will you feel? Remember, for you to materialise the loving relationship you want, you must first imagine it. What is the last thing that has to happen so that you know you've achieved your goal? Are you arm and arm looking out at your garden? Are you on honeymoon? Are you cuddling up on the couch? Are you in bed? What are you seeing? What are you hearing? Most importantly, what are you feeling? This spurs your unconscious mind to begin actively creating what you have been strongly imagining without you even noticing it.

Through your imagination you can consciously instruct your unconscious mind. You can send instructions about what you want by imagining events and visualising goals, and your subconscious mind will work to make them happen.

The instructions you give can be in the form of words, feelings or pictures. Professional golfers regularly use visualisation to mentally rehearse how they want to perform, by picturing themselves successfully completing their rounds, overcoming difficulties and winning championships. Other professional sports competitors do the same. For example, a football player might see a football striking his foot at just the right angle, at just the perfect moment to score or set up the perfect goal. Studies consistently show that this form of visualisation dramatically improves performance in many spheres of life.

And the same thing can work for you. What is important is that you imagine what it would feel like to have your goal. How great would it feel if you were in a loving relationship with the partner of your dreams? Make sure you are feeling the feelings of joy and happiness. Then double those feelings, treble them! Step out of your body and see yourself in the scene. Take a deep breath and breathe out energy into this picture. Do this three more times. Now act as if you've already achieved your goal. Act as if getting your wonderful relationship is a foregone conclusion.

Tell me, what would you do if you knew you couldn't fail? If you knew that somewhere in the future you had already achieved your goal, how would you act now? If you stopped to consider this question even for a moment, you have done what all really successful people have always done – used their imagination to visualise and become excited about their end product. They used their imagination and ability to daydream and to stimulate the creativity within them. This state of creativity is absolutely vital because, for anything to happen in the real world, it first has to happen in the imagination.

4. What will it achieve for you or allow you to do?

State all the benefits you'll receive from the desired results. What will achieving the goal enable you to do? How will your life be affected?

5. Is the goal self-initiated?

Is this goal only for you, or is it a goal initiated by others who believe they know what's good for you? Are you setting the goal out of a sense of duty or obligation, or because you think it's expected of you? Make sure it's your goal, initiated by you.

6. *Where, when, how and with whom do you want to accomplish this goal?*

Where, specifically, do you want your result to take place? Will it be close to home, near your family and friends, or will it be far away? In your own street or on a mountaintop in Tibet?

When do you want to achieve your goal? Specify a day, month, and year.

With whom or in what context? You may wish to specify the social circle that you want to achieve your goal, for example, your co-workers or people who share your hobby. If your goal is to meet the ideal man or woman and form a relationship, you can also specify the characteristics you'd like that person to have.

7. *What resources do you need?*

What do you have now and what do you need to achieve your goal? Have you ever accomplished this goal before? Do you know anyone who has already succeeded in doing so? What did they do? How do they act? What are their beliefs? Can you talk to them or read about their experiences? What personal qualities do you have or do you need to develop to achieve this goal? Think of all your personal skills and capabilities. Can you act as if you've achieved the goal?

8. *Is the goal responsible and ecological?*

What are the consequences of achieving it? For what purpose do you want to achieve this goal? What will you gain or lose if you achieve it? What will happen if you achieve it? What won't happen if you achieve it? What will happen if you don't achieve it? What won't happen if you don't achieve it?

9. *Create an action plan*

Once you've examined your desired goal using these questions you're ready to act. You can use the questions and your answers to plan the steps you'll take to achieve your goal.

Set Your Dream Goals Exercise

Sit down with a pen and paper and use the nine keys to formulate your relationship goal. Then list ten actions you'll take to achieve the goal and the date by which you'll complete each step.

1. What, specifically, do you want?
2. Where are you now? Describe your present situation.
3. What will you see, hear and feel when you have the relationship of your dreams?
4. How will you know when you have it?
5. What will you gain if you achieve this goal or what will it allow you to do?
6. Is this goal only for you? If not, who else is it for?
7. Where, when, how, and with whom do you want to achieve it?
8. What resources do you have now, and what do you need to achieve your goal?Have you ever achieved this goal before? Do you know anyone who has? Can you act as if you have it?
9. For what purpose do you want to accomplish this goal? What will you gain or lose if you achieve it? What will happen if you achieve it? What won't happen if you achieve it? What will happen if you don't achieve it? What won't happen if you don't achieve it?

Now write down exactly which steps you'll take to achieve your goal and exactly when you'll take each action (day/month/year).

Action
1._____
    When? ____/____/____

Action
2.

    When? ____/____/____

Action
3.

    When? ____/____/____

Action
4.

    When? ____/____/____

Action
5.

    When? ____/____/____

Action
6.

    When? ____/____/____

Action
7.

When? ____ / ____ / ____

Action
8._____

When? ____ / ____ / ____

Action
9.

_____

When? ____ / ____ / ____

Action
10.

_____

When? ____ / ____ / ____

Fast Track Your Love Goal

Now that you are clear about what you want, you can attract it to you even more quickly, by knowing the *essence* of what this relationship or person will bring to you. The essence is essentially what you think the relationship will give you. What needs would it satisfy? What qualities will it bring into your life? How would it satisfy you? To increase your powers of attraction you need to become familiar with the essence of what you want. This means that when you attract your relationship, it will be one that really satisfies you and brings you joy and happiness.

Knowing the essence of what you want and attracting it to you.

When you know the essence of what you want, you make it possible to come to you in many ways. For example, if the essence of what you want from a relationship is love, happiness and excitement, you might be able to discover many ways to create this before you get your relationship. In fact, using other ways to bring more of these qualities into your life will in turn increase your chances of getting them through a relationship. If you don't know the essence of what you want, you can attract a person who is completely unsuitable, does not meet your needs, is unable to love, or is dull and boring.

So you really need to get specific about what you want a new relationship to bring you. This could be love, sex, security, joy, happiness, fun, laughter, excitement and so on. Ask yourself 'How would I know if I were happy? What would I need to feel secure? What do I get excited about?'

Once you are clear about the essence of what you want, learn to recognise it when it does come. Your ideal person may come from unexpected places or invitations.

To successfully attract love into your life, focus on creating what you want, not on getting rid of what you don't want. You'd be surprised at how many people tell you what they don't want when you ask them to describe how they want their lives to be. If there are things in your life that you don't want, then describe as clearly as possible what you would replace them with.

You must also be sure that what you are hoping for is something you can imagine having. You must believe that it is possible to have the relationship of your dreams. Some of you may want to take a little time to build you confidence, so that you believe it is possible. All you need to do is imagine that you are enjoying the company of the opposite sex, that you are interacting with men and having fun, being interested, feeling attractive, and confident. As you imagine this, it will soon materialise in your life and each success will build upon another. Your subconscious mind has a stronger and stronger belief that you are attractive and can bring the right sort of person into your life.

As you experience the little successes, you develop a belief and you just 'know' that it is possible to create that wonderful relationship you thought was impossible when you began. It is that inner knowing that it is possible, or even probable, that you will get what you want, which is crucial to you achieving your relationship goal.

Once you have decided that your goal is worth getting, you

may not have to put much energy into it, but be willing to do so if necessary. Once you start focussing on the essence of what you want, be aware that you are going to get what you ask for more easily than you expect. Show appreciation and congratulate yourself when something you want comes into your life, be this a date, an invitation, a holiday, a new friend or a relationship. Be sure to recognise that you have drawn these things to you and know that they all indicate you are getting closer to your goal.

Finding the Essence of What I Want

Think about the relationship you want to attract into your life, and the partner of your dreams.

1. Write down exactly what it is you want to create. Be as specific as possible.
2. What more can you ask that would make it even better?
3. How much energy, time and commitment would it take? What is the level of intention?
4. What quality do you hope this relationship will bring into your life? (Love, joy, happiness, peace of mind, security, excitement, fun).
5. List five ways you can experience this quality right now.

Being absolutely clear about what you want is essential for drawing a relationship into your life in a way that really does fulfil and satisfy you. You need to attract not only the thing itself (the relationship or the person) but also the essence of what you hope they will bring you.

Act now!

To achieve your goal quickly and easily, you need to focus on it and you need to *act*. Firstly, you must make sure that your actions are not contradicting your desires.

There is a wonderful, yet all too familiar, story retold in *The Secret* by Rhonda Byrne of a woman who wanted to attract her perfect partner into her life. The woman did everything right. She worked on herself. She knew precisely what she wanted in a man, she made a list of all his qualities and characteristics, and she used her imagination to visualise her perfect partner in her life. But in spite of taking all these actions there was still no sign of him. Then she came home one day and noticed she had unconsciously parked her car in the middle of the garage. It suddenly dawned on her, that her behaviour was contradicting what she wanted. By parking her care in the middle of the garage she was telling her unconscious mind and the universe that she had no room in her life for her perfect partner's car or her perfect partner. Her actions said loud and clear that she did not believe she was going to receive what she most wanted.

On realising this she immediately cleaned up her garage and parked her car to one side. Expectantly, she left space on the other side for her perfect partner's car. She then looked at her house and found that in her bedroom, her wardrobe was crammed full of clothes. There wasn't any space for her perfect partner's clothes. So she cleared out some of her wardrobe and made room. She had also been sleeping in the middle of her bed, and so she began sleeping on one side, leaving space for her future partner.

The woman told her story one evening to entrepreneur and author Mike Dooley at a dinner party. Sitting next to her at the table was her perfect partner. By changing her behaviour, clearing out her clutter, making room in her life and acting as if she had already received her perfect partner, he arrived in her life, and Rhonda Byrne tells us they are now happily married.

So take a good look at your actions, have you made room in your life for your perfect partner? Do your actions and desires complement each other, or contradict each other?

The next thing you need to do is get out there and meet people! Take a good look at your social life. Are you meeting the type of people you want to meet? Are you having fun and enjoying yourself? If not, change things. Decide what you enjoy doing most and go out there and do it!

Create a social diary. Get out and meet people and start

networking. Make the effort. Begin to expand your social horizons and engagements. It doesn't matter whether you are going out with a man or not, it is a great thing to have a full social life. You will have a far greater chance and choice of finding your dream partner if you are out and about. You are not going to meet the man of your dreams by staying at home. Don't expect him to come knocking at your front door.

It's important that you begin to go to environments that are frequented by the sort of people you want to meet. Sharing similar interests or values with the people you meet, means it is more likely that one of them will be the right person for you. If you are being serious and not only looking for someone who is single, but who is going to meet your deepest desire (a long-term committed relationship), you need to think about being in the types of environments where you will meet just that sort of person.

If you are going to the same old places and doing the same old things, and they are not getting you any closer to the loving relationship you desire, then do something else! Try something new and get out of your comfort zone.

In his best selling business book *Who moved my cheese?*, Spencer Johnson explains a key difference between humans and rats. If rats are doing something and they discover that it isn't working, they stop doing it and try something else. If humans discover what they're doing isn't working, they look for someone to blame and often repeat the same actions or patterns over and over again! If you want to get different results in your life, you'll need to step outside your comfort zone and do something different.

Similarly, if you are in a relationship or just starting one and you are not getting the results you want, do something different. If you always do what you've always done, you'll get the same results. So change you're behaviour. What can you do if you don't feel valued or appreciated or feel taken for granted in a relationship? Even if you are not in a relationship yet, this is worth knowing for your future happiness.

There are two different ways you can act in a relationship, the way of the 'nice girl' and the way of the 'Goddess'. In the following scenarios, who would you prefer to be? Imagine you have been dating your new boyfriend for several months. Then consider the outcome of each of the behaviours.

Situation 1: Your new man calls you and just expects you to be at home.

Nice girl: If the nice girl goes out, she lets him know where she is going to be, who she'll be with and when she'll be back. The outcome is that he takes her for granted.

The Goddess: The Goddess doesn't tell him where she is every minute of the day. She allows him to wonder where she is every now and then. This outcome is that this keeps him interested and a little on his toes!

Situation 2: He says he'll call at a certain time and then phones you four hours later.

Nice girl: The nice girl shouts at him, tells him he should have called and she was worried. The outcome is that he thinks she is hooked and will always be hanging around waiting.

The Goddess: The Goddess doesn't get upset so easily or at least she 'acts as if' she doesn't. This means it is not easy to know what is in her mind. She may or she may not pick up the phone. This makes him think about her and miss her.

Situation 3: He is very late for a date and keeps you waiting.

Nice girl: The nice girl waits, calls him several times on his mobile, and tells him how long she's been waiting and he should 'value her more'. The outcome is that he takes her for granted.

The Goddess: The Goddess waits half an hour and then makes other plans. She goes away and treats herself. The outcome is that he worries that he's 'blown it'.

The big difference in these situations isn't as much how the man treats you, as how you treat yourself. The Goddess lets him know, without any words, that she values herself and her life. Because she values and respects herself, he will value and respect her too.

If you have confidence and respect for yourself, others will pick up on this and treat you well. But, if you have low self-esteem, others reflect your lack of self-worth back to you and may treat you poorly. Feeling better about yourself starts with you, no one can make you feel better about yourself. Your boyfriend or partner cannot satisfy the needs you should be satisfying yourself.

Linda Field in *Weekend Love Coach* gives us some good advice when she says 'get a life then get a man'. If you do this, you will be emotionally independent before you begin your relationship. You will be able to stand on your own two feet and you'll not make unrealistic or unreasonable demands of your partner. Your new relationship will, therefore, have a much better chance of growing into a deep, loving, supportive, committed relationship. Self-confidence begins at home; it comes from within and leads to confidence in a relationship.

And remember, go easy on yourself, no matter what you do and what happens. There is no such thing as failure, only feedback. You learn from your experiences and will do things differently the next time. Take everything as a learning experience.

You have only failed when you decide to stop learning. Until then, every response you get, every reaction is valuable information that can be used to tell you whether your actions are taking you closer to, of further away, from what you want. In fact, successful people understand that you achieve success when you are finished with failing. Studies of successful entrepreneurs show that people who've 'made it' have one thing in common – they've made more mistakes than people who haven't. Every mistake or failure is an opportunity for learning, cleverly disguised. So relax! Whatever the outcome of your actions, you will gain. Either things will go exactly the way you want or you will be more confident in similar circumstances in the future.

It is only natural that most people perform best when they are free from anxiety and relaxed. But how is it possible to keep from freezing up or worrying when you are in a nerve-racking situation. The answer: you can't! So if you feel you haven't made a good first impression, or things aren't going exactly the way you'd planned, don't feel bad. Think of it as a learning experience, and know that you'll feel so much more confident with similar situations in the future. No matter what the outcome, there are always some benefits. You will always win, either you'll get just what you wanted (by design or accident), or you'll gain valuable experience.

Get Motivated and Stay Motivated

To act and go for the relationship you really want, you must feel motivated, really motivated. You'll only feel really motivated and have the necessary energy to get your result if you truly *value* your goal. Consciously we might think we value a loving, supportive relationship but unconsciously our values could be working against us. Indeed, I have noticed that many of my clients' unconscious values had prevented them from getting the loving relationship they wanted.

You'll have noticed that you're motivated to do some things and distinctly unconcerned about others. The ones you feel motivated about are the ones that help you to satisfy a value that you consider important. Values are often unconscious and are usually abstract concepts, such as honesty, love, loyalty, compassion and integrity. Values help you decide what's important and help you to evaluate your actions. Your values will tell you whether what you did was right or wrong, good or bad.

Your values determine how you act and how you spend your time, so your top five relationship values will tell you how you automatically and unconsciously choose to spend your time in that area of your life. Here's the critical thing. If the goals you've set for your relationship are aligned with your relationship values, you'll unconsciously take action to achieve your goal. It's automatic and easy. If you set a goal that is not aligned with your values, you won't spend all your time unconsciously achieving that goal. It will be much more difficult for you.

How do you ensure that your relationship values are in

47

alignment with your goals and are working for you? The key is to find out what your relationship values are by asking yourself one simple question over and over: 'What's important to me about having a relationship?' You're looking for abstractions. For example, if I asked you what was important to you about having a relationship and you said, 'To feel that someone is there for me', I would ask, 'What's important to you about feeling that someone is there for you?' And if you said, 'Oh, just to feel safe', I would say, 'What's important to you about feeling safe?' And if you said, 'To be secure because security is important', I would write down 'security'. So listen out for single-word abstractions, such as 'companionship', 'love' and 'security' and so on.

The following exercise will enable you to discover the unconscious values which have been determining how you feel and behave in a relationship.

Unlocking Your Driving Force - Discovering Your Relationship Values

1. Take a sheet of paper and ask yourself, 'What's important to me about having a relationship?' Quickly write down whatever comes to mind. Ask yourself, 'What else is important to me about having a relationship? What else, what else...?' and so on. Write down all the words and phrases you come up with until you feel you've exhausted the subject.
2. Rest for a few moments, then ask yourself again 'What's important to me about having a relationship?' You'll find that more words pop into your head. Write those down too.
3. Look at all the values you've written and ask yourself, 'If I could have only one value for a relationship what would it be? What's most important to me?' Write your answer on a separate piece of paper.
4. Ask yourself, 'If I could have only one more value out of all of these, what would it be?' Note that one underneath your response to question 3. 'If I could have one more, which one would it be?' Repeat this step until you've elicited five values.

Well done, you've discovered your relationship values. Read them back to yourself and ask, 'If I had a relationship that satisfied all these values would I be happy?' These values are what drives and motivates you, and the goal you've set for yourself must be in alignment with them. If you find that your values and goals are aligned, great! If not, simply set an equally compelling goal that's aligned to your values. You'll find that achieving it is easy. Go for it!

Your Purpose in Life – your compass

Now that you have set a precise, clearly defined love goal and you understand what is truly important to you in a relationship – your relationship values - there is one more thing you need to know to make achieving your goal as easy as possible. Strange as it may sound, you need to understand what your purpose in life is. Why? Because your life's purpose will also determine how easy or hard attaining your relationship goals will be.

Your life's purpose is your internal compass. When your actions are in accordance with your life's purpose, things seem to happen easily and you're at your happiest. When your actions are at odds with your purpose, relationships and life are a struggle and you're not happy. Think back, do you remember a time when things came easily, when things seemed to happen naturally and the pieces fell into place with almost no effort? If so, you succeeded and felt happy at the time because your actions were aligned to your life's purpose.

Indeed, the easiest way of assessing whether what you're doing is aligned with your life's purpose, is to see whether things are happening easily for you and you're happy, or whether life seems a struggle and you're not happy. When the goals you set are aligned to your life's purpose, you'll find that achieving them is fun and easy. Knowing your life's purpose also helps you to make better decisions in your relationships. If you're presented with a range of options, knowing your life's purpose will help you make the best choice naturally.

Knowing your purpose in life is also the key to getting your love spells to work, as they will ensure you are permanently motivated and never bored. Your life's purpose is a *major* goal that you'll spend your life pursuing, so let's discover your life's purpose.

You won't be aware of your life's purpose because it's held deep in your unconscious mind. Use the following process to allow the cosmos and your unconscious mind to tell you what your purpose is. You may think the questions I'm going to ask next are rather strange, but serious consideration of these questions is also crucial if you're going to achieve the relationship you want easily and quickly.

Have you ever wondered if you have a purpose in life? What your life is about? Whether it has a meaning? Everyone has a purpose. However, most people haven't given it much thought and few people know what theirs is. Now you can. You'll need to set aside fifteen to twenty minutes to complete this process.

Divining Your Purpose in Life

Step 1
Go through the entire list of words below and circle all the items that give you strong positive feelings, like really happy, excited, loved, content, confident, or powerful and so on. Which ones make you feel really good? Then go back and pick the top three or four themes (topics) that you find most important or meaningful. Remember, there are no correct answers, and it's up to you to decide what meaning each word or phrase has for you.

Achieving your goals
Being happy
Gaining recognition
Earning money
Building something
Loving someone (others)
Being loved, being accepted

Winning
Finding the good in others
Waiting until the last minute
Having prestige
Gaining the approval of

Becoming an expert
Being popular
Being competent
Being independent
Risking
Being different and still fitting in
Being your best
Reaching your potential
Finding excitement
Being a leader
Learning, gaining wisdom
Gaining mastery
Seeking adventure
Making a worthwhile contribution
Having power or authority
Fully expressing yourself
Developing people or things
Increasing your effectiveness
others
Creating something
Getting things done
Doing good
Dominating
Being unique
Being the best
Gaining security, safety
Being in control
Having fun
Working hard
Having influence over
others
Experiencing life to its
fullest
Making a difference
Seeing how much you
can get away with

(If a word or phrase that isn't on this list comes to mind, please add it.)

Step 2
Go back to a time when you felt that you really accomplished something, when you felt joy, happiness and a sense of accomplishment. Go back to that time now. See through your eyes, hear through your ears. What are you seeing? What are you hearing? Really feel that sense of accomplishment. Great. Keep that feeling, and list at least one accomplishment in each age category that gave you a sense of joy, regardless of what others thought at the time. Answer questions 1 to 4 to further identify the important aspects of each accomplishment. (If you don't come up with an answer right away, quickly move on.)
What accomplishment gave you the greatest sense of joy, happiness and achievement when you were aged:

0–12 years?

What was the activity? _____
What did you actually do? _____

What, specifically, was the sense of joy? _____

What abilities did the accomplishment demonstrate? _____

What was the general subject matter? _____
What were the circumstances? _____

What were the relationships to other people and things? _____

13–17 years?

What was the activity? _____
What did you actually do? _____

What, specifically, was the sense of joy? _____

What abilities did the accomplishment demonstrate? _____

What was the general subject matter? _____
What were the circumstances? _____

What were the relationships to other people and things? _____

18–22 years?

What was the activity? _____
What did you actually do? _____

What, specifically, was the sense of joy? _____

What abilities did the accomplishment demonstrate? _____

What was the general subject matter? _____
What were the circumstances? _____

What were the relationships to other people and things?_____

23–30 years?

What was the activity? _____
What did you actually do? _____

What, specifically, was the sense of joy? _____

What abilities did the accomplishment demonstrate? _____

What was the general subject matter? _____
What were the circumstances? _____

What were the relationships to other people and things?_____

31–40 years?

What was the activity? _____
What did you actually do? _____

What, specifically, was the sense of joy? _____

What abilities did the accomplishment demonstrate? _____

What was the general subject matter? _____
What were the circumstances? _____

What were the relationships to other people and things? _____

_____

41–50 years?

What was the activity? _____

What did you actually do? _____

What, specifically, was the sense of joy? _____

What abilities did the accomplishment demonstrate?

What was the general subject matter? _____

What were the circumstances? _____

What were the relationships to other people and things?

_____

51–60 years?

What was the activity? _____

What did you actually do? _____

What, specifically, was the sense of joy? _____

What abilities did the accomplishment demonstrate?

What was the general subject matter? _____

What were the circumstances? _____

What were the relationships to other people and things?

_____

61+ years?

What was the activity? _____

What did you actually do? _____

_____

What, specifically, was the sense of joy? _____

_____

What abilities did the accomplishment demonstrate?

_____

What was the general subject matter? _____

What were the circumstances? _____

_____

What were the relationships to other people and things?

_____

Step 3
Answer the following summary questions (take your time to consider each question carefully):

1. Throughout your life, which activity has consistently produced the greatest sense of joy? _____

2. What skills or abilities do you most like to use or demonstrate?

_____

_____

3. What do you most like about yourself? _____

_____

_____

4. What patterns do you observe in your answers so far?

_____

_____

Step 4
Complete the following survey in as much detail as possible on a separate sheet of paper, if necessary, to create a description of yourself when you're demonstrating your purpose.

1. What are you doing when you experience the greatest sense of self-fulfilment? _____

2. Who are you being when you experience the greatest sense of joy?

3. Describe the visual images you see when you're being this person.

4. Describe what it feels like to be this person.

5. Describe the things you say to yourself when you're being this person.

6. Describe the conversations you have with other people when you're being this person.

Devote some time to these important questions and revise your answers periodically as you make new and important discoveries about yourself and your sense of purpose.

Step 5
Take the information from steps 1 through 4 and write a statement of purpose using words that cause you to feel deeply about what your life is about. Don't worry about grammatical correctness. Your statement of purpose can have as little as one word or as many as you need to create a strong emotional feeling deep within you. The key is to come up with a theme, a definition of the driving force in your life that you can review regularly and that provides you with a strong emotional charge each time you read it.

Think about this theme over the next few days and add to it or tidy it up. Let it be absolutely right for you. Then type it up, laminate it and put it on your desk or carry it in your pocket. Next time you wake up and think, 'Why am I doing this?' Look at your life's purpose and ask, 'Am I living on purpose?' If you're not, do something about it. Live on purpose.

Now you know how to achieve the goals you've set

What will happen if you set a clear, compelling goal to achieve the relationship of your dreams? Your goal will provide you with the precise destination you want to reach. Simply by focusing on this destination each day you'll be well on the path to achieving it. There is someone (or perhaps there are several men) out there who are exactly right for you. By focusing on your love goal and what you want, you are drawing them closer to you.

Remember that there are men out there waiting for someone to love too. The amazing thing is that you can be that someone! All you have to do is focus on your goal, know how it will feel when you are in a loving relationship and take action, no matter how small right now. Very soon other people will be reflecting back to you the love and good feelings you are sending out. One of them will be the lover of your dreams.

Because you've given your unconscious mind clear, positive instructions and it knows where you want to be, it will immediately work in often unnoticed ways to bring about what you desire. What will happen if you align your goal with your deeply held values and your purpose in life? Because it's in accordance with your values and your purpose in life, the things you want will happen easily, and as if by magic your life will be transformed.

Your Practical Magic for Level 2

1. Set a compelling relationship goal. Then set goals for your career, health and fitness, money and personal development. It's helpful to set goals in all areas of your life, as this makes you an even more balanced, confident and ultimately attractive person. As you set goals for your career, health, fitness and personal

development, watch for improvements in your social life and finding the relationship you want.

2.   Discover your relationship values and ensure that the goals you set are in alignment with these values.

3.   Discover your purpose in life and ensure that all the goals you set help you to work towards your purpose.

Well done. You may now proceed to Level 3.

Level 3

Get Emotional Freedom –
Divining Love and Happiness

What if you knew how to control your emotional state? What if you could choose not to have troubling feelings? What if you could decide how you feel in any situation? Imagine what it would be like if you could feel positive, happy and confident whenever you wanted to? Most people think that events and people outside their control cause their emotional state when, in reality, we create our own feelings. In this Level you'll learn how to choose your emotional state.

What Makes Us Feel the Way We Do?

Have you ever woken up feeling unhappy and in low spirits for no reason you can think of? Have you noticed how these feelings have affected your whole day, what you do, or how you get on with other people? But that's just human, isn't it? We all have these feelings, don't we?

Often we believe that we are the only ones who feel the way we do. Yet at one time or another all of us will have felt angry, sad, frightened, or jealous. We'll all have felt happy and loving too. Everyone has feelings. What is important to understand is that our feelings are exactly that, they are *our* feelings.

When my clients first talk about their problems they'll often say 'He made me feel sad', or 'She made me angry', or 'I felt jealous because he did this or she did that'. I can relate to this because in the past I've also said that another person's actions were the cause of my feelings. But who really is responsible for how we feel and how we respond to people's words and actions?

If an individual really had the power to make people feel certain emotions, then they would be able to create and predict other people's reactions at will. Yet, this is notoriously difficult. If you asked one hundred people how they felt after, say, watching a programme about Africa on TV, you would get as many different responses. Similarly, if you asked a hundred people at a conference how they felt after getting feedback about their presentation, you would again get a hundred different responses. The responses would depend on how each person interpreted the comments which in turn would be based on their past experience and beliefs about the situation and themselves. While one person may get angry at your words another might find them informative.

It is our interpretation and meaning that we give to the words and actions of others that causes us to feel the way we do. This means we are responsible for our own feelings. If we blame other people for 'making us' feel bad or good, we are giving away our power and denying that we have a choice in every situation.

If we accept that we somehow create our feelings and responses then we can also change them.

Understanding and Controlling Your Emotions

Your emotional state affects your actions. When you feel happy, the happiness radiates in your body language. You smile, you walk with your head up and you're open to other people. It's like magic. Have you noticed how, when you feel happy, the world seems a friendlier place? More people seem to say 'hello' or wave; maybe you chat pleasantly with somebody at work or at the shops. Often, you'll talk to strangers. Not surprisingly, this optimism attracts others to you and widens your social circle. Things seem to go right. Your good mood may even trigger memories of happy times, making you feel even better. It is almost as if there is an enchantment around you. You interact better with other people and are more likely to attract good friends and prospective partners and spouses if you cultivate optimism and happiness. When you feel calm and confident it's also easier to think clearly and rationally.

Conversely, the more uptight and intense we are, the more disruptive and difficult our thinking becomes. We can think that someone has insulted us or belittled us when that was not their intention at all. If we were in a happy mood what they said may not have bothered us at all. Our mood colours our interpretation of every interaction.

If someone speaks to you in a way that you *perceive* to be patronising or condescending, you may feel humiliated and upset. However, you are putting your own interpretation on how they spoke to you. In doing so your reaction is very likely to be a reflection of your own feelings. If, on the other hand, you had been feeling good about yourself, you might not have let the way they spoke to you to bother you at all.

Our emotional state can affect our capabilities in every area of life. Take our career. Say I have an important job interview. I have rehearsed the interview many times and I am able to sail through questions when no one is with me. But when I'm at the interview with a panel of five people I might be so nervous and uptight that I forget what I'd planned to say and don't respond well to the questions. Yet I know the answers and I know my stuff. I may be suffering from 'interview anxiety' that can diminish my performance by as much as 20 to 30 percent. Some people get so tongue tied at interviews that they don't portray themselves in a good light at all. They may appear incapable and incompetent, yet they aren't. All they need to do is manage their emotional state, and do something which will reduce their anxiety.

How well you learn also depends on your emotional state, so does how you perform and interact. You naturally learn more, and quickly and easily when you're interested and curious, fascinated and excited, than when you're bored, anxious, hostile and listless.

Whatever feelings you have at a particular time will attract more of the same. Have you ever felt sad and noticed how that feeling brought to mind other times when you felt the same way?

Have you noticed that when you feel irritated and annoyed at one thing, lots of other things seem to go wrong that day? You had an argument with a colleague at work, a shop assistant was rude to you, and when you got home you couldn't help but feel annoyed when a friend telephoned to tell you about all the problems she's been having with her partner. What you feel and what you focus your attention on will bring more of the same to you. This lesson is important to learn well.

I know you're asking, 'How can I not feel a particular way?' 'How can I change the way I feel?' 'What can I do about it?'

For the rest of this Level I'll give you the tools to create the best, most productive, feelings you can have in any situation. How you use them is up to you.

Here's the next thing you can do to begin gaining control over your emotions. Simply close your eyes right now and imagine yourself lying in a hammock strung across two palm trees on a beautiful white beach. Be in your own body, look through your own eyes at the waves coming in to the shore and retreating again. Feel the warmth of the sun on your skin and hear the waves sweeping up the beach and returning to the sea. When you're inside your body looking through your own eyes you're what psychologists would term as *associated*. Notice how you feel.

Now imagine the same scene but this time float up out of your body looking down at yourself. See yourself lying in the hammock. Fly around and see yourself from different angles. Then float back down again into your body and open your eyes. When you see yourself in a picture, looking from the outside, you're *dissociated*.

Being associated (in your own body, seeing through your own eyes) brings up strong feelings because you're in touch with bodily sensations and feelings. When you're dissociated you're out of touch with your body. Although you still have feelings they're less intense because they're *about* what you see rather than part of the experience.

Being associated is good for enjoying pleasant experiences, happy memories, practicing a skill and paying attention. Being dissociated is good for reviewing the past, thinking about unpleasant memories and learning from your experiences.

The first simple step to managing your emotions is to be associated when you think of pleasant memories and to be dissociated when you think of uncomfortable memories.

Our Emotional Triggers

Many sensations trigger specific emotional states. Do you have, or remember having, a song that reminds you of someone in your past and brings back some of the feelings you had for that person? Or does a particular song remind you of a certain time and place, maybe on holiday? Does it bring back the good feelings you enjoyed then? Does it make you feel happy and warm? Smells can also trigger strong emotions. A certain perfume or aftershave can immediately remind you of a particular person and the feelings you had for him or her. A particular person can trigger certain emotions in you. Have you ever felt your heart sink when you heard a certain person's voice or saw them approaching you? Somehow, that person's face or sound of their voice always triggers something in you that makes you feel bad. The person is a trigger for feeling angry or unhappy. Sights and sounds and smells that trigger memories or emotions are called 'anchors'.

The key to gaining control over your emotions is to use the 'anchor spell'. That is, to become aware of your anchors and choose to create powerful *new* anchors that you can use any time you want. Using your happiest and most confident moments to create new anchors will help you to feel great and behave in a way that can get you the results you want.

How to Cast the 'Anchor' Spell and Create Emotional Freedom

Being able to choose how you feel and change your emotional state will help you gain emotional freedom and create the happy, successful relationship you're looking for. Of course, it doesn't mean you'll never feel sad or angry, but it does mean you'll be able to handle those emotions and choose how you respond. Being in a negative emotional state from time to time is a normal part of everyday life. Simply be aware of the state you're in. Next, realise that you have a choice. You can choose to stay in this state or you can choose to change it. If you want to change it you can do so in a number of ways.

Breaking the Old Spell (The Negative Emotional Cycle) 1

Step 1
If you start off in a negative emotional state, like sadness or anger, happiness and contentment may seem a long way off. In this situation, you first have to break or interrupt the negative state you're in by abruptly distracting your attention. For example, if you're sitting, suddenly stand up, spine straight, shoulders back, and briskly walk around the room. Move! Look out the window. Be drawn to something interesting. Be distracted by a noise. Touch some fabric. Anything that interrupts your pattern of thinking will move you into a more neutral emotional state.

Step 2
Sit comfortably with your spine straight, shoulders down and relaxed, head nicely balanced on top of the spine. Breathe deeply through your nose, fill your lungs with air and breathe out slowly through your nose. Make sure every particle of air is expelled before you breathe in. Do this five times. Relax the muscles of your face, beginning with your forehead. Relax your eyebrows, your eyes, and your cheeks. Feel all the little muscles in and around your mouth relax. Relax your neck and shoulders and down your back to your pelvis and tailbone. Then go back to the throat muscles. Relax. Let the relaxation flow down your arms to your elbows, through your elbows to your wrists, from your wrists to your palms, through your palms to your fingertips. Relax.Now come back again to the relaxed muscles of your throat

and feel the relaxation flow down into your chest, your abdomen, your pelvic area and hips. Feel the relaxation flow down into your thighs, through your knees, around and inside your calves and deep into your feet and toes. Your whole body is relaxed. Good.

Breaking the Old Spell to Get Emotional Freedom

Emotional Freedom Technique (EFT) is an amazing tool developed by Gary Craig. Craig modified and simplified the procedures used in Thought Field Therapy, originally created by Dr. Roger Callahan. These techniques have been subject to many studies and have been found to substantially reduce negative emotions such as sadness, fear, anger, anxiety and stress, and to promote a sense of calmness and relaxation. They increase serotonin in the body (the chemicals which make you feel happy) and decrease adrenaline and noradrenalin (the chemicals responsible for stress).

Gary Craig argues that negative emotions are fuelled and maintained by a disruption of the body's energy system. A negative emotion is created by a disturbing or distressing thought or memory. This in turn causes a 'short circuit' or blockage in the body's energy system, which in turn leads to an upsetting emotion like sadness.

What this Emotional Freedom Technique allows you to do is release this 'blockage' by tapping on specific acupuncture points in your body. The result of tapping in the sequence I am about to show you is to re-programme the way your mind interprets and responds to stress, thereby calming your emotions. You will begin by focussing on the negative emotion you want to be free of, such as sadness, anger, guilt etc. You will have to concentrate on this feeling for a few minutes while you follow my instructions.

It doesn't matter whether you tap using your left hand or your right hand, or which side of the body you tap. Either side or either hand will be equally effective. So just do whatever feels comfortable to you.

The Emotional Freedom Technique

Before doing this technique be sure to read through the instructions fully so that you know exactly what you are doing.

1. I'd like you to focus on your negative emotion such as anger, fear, sadness, jealousy or guilt.

2. Now on a scale of 1 to 10 I want you to rate the emotion, with 1 being the lowest (not sad at all) and 10 (really, really sad). This is quite important, because at the end you want to know how much you've reduced it by.

3. Now we are going to create a statement for you to say out loud. It is very important that you concentrate on the statement and that you really mean it. Your intention to rid yourself of the emotion is what makes this technique work so effectively. So here is the statement: 'Even though, I feel sad (or whatever negative emotion you've identified), I choose to let it go now, and I deeply love and accept t myself'. Repeat this three times while taking your two fingers and rubbing the middle point of your right or left breast. You will notice a spot that feels tender, this is called the 'sore spot'.

4. Next take two fingers and tap on the following points 7 or 8 times while repeating this shorter statement: 'I choose to let the (sadness or other emotion) go now'.

> Crown of head
> Above the eyebrow
> Side of eye
> Under eye
> Under nose
> Under lip
> Under collar bone
> Under arm (six inches down from armpit)

5. Take a deep breath. Now check on a scale of 1 to 10, what number is the emotion (e.g. sadness)? If it hasn't completely gone, repeat this process until it does.

Now you can proceed immediately to improving your emotional state by casting the Instant Feel-Good spell. Here's how to do it.

Instant Feel Good Spell

Step 1. Choose the emotional state you want to be in. Here are some good ones:
- Feeling ecstatically happy
- Feeling loved
- Feeling powerful
- Feeling confident
- Feeling that you can have whatever you want

Think of any constructive emotions you like, but make sure they're intense and vibrant.

Step 2. Sit up with your spine straight, your head balanced on top of your spine, your shoulders down and relaxed. Breathe deeply, letting the corners of your mouth turn up. 'Acting as if' you're already in this state, smile.

Close your eyes and go back to a time when you felt so ecstatically happy that you wanted to fall down laughing. Float down into your body and see what you saw, hear what you heard, notice what you noticed and really feel as ecstatically happy as you did then. Now make the colours brighter and the sounds louder and let the feeling intensify. Now double the feeling, treble it.

Step 3. As these wonderful feelings intensify, squeeze the thumb and middle finger of your right hand together. Keep squeezing firmly and when you feel the feeling beginning to subside, let go. Good.

Step 4. Repeat steps 1 to 3 three times, feeling ecstatically happy. Open your eyes. Stand up and look around the room. Take three big, deep breaths. Sit down.

Step 5. Squeeze the thumb and middle finger of your right

hand together again. You'll feel the ecstatic happiness rise up within you. Whenever you wish to feel happy all you have to do is press together your thumb and middle finger of your right hand.

You can create a huge emotional resource anchor for yourself by repeating steps 1 to 5 with all the positive emotions you want to generate in yourself. Follow the same procedure to feel totally loved, totally powerful, and totally confident. Do it now. All those wonderful feelings will be at your fingertips. And you can use this anchor any time you want to feel fantastic.

What is more, if you're having a wonderful time right now and something makes you go into fits of laughter, you can anchor it! That is, simply squeeze together the thumb and middle finger of your right hand. Doing this whenever you're enjoying great feelings will give you the most powerful and productive anchor that you can ever imagine, and you can use it whenever you want.

Now you know how to generate fantastic feelings whenever you want to. What's more, the more you use this technique the more powerful these feelings will become. Imagine calling up feelings of happiness, joy, motivation, and excitement whenever you needed to be happy or motivated. Imagine how you'll attract people to you, how you'll talk to them and how much they will enjoy your company all because you can get into your most productive happy state whenever you want. You'll get much more from socialising whether you're going to a party, a pub, or a convention by being motivated and happy.

Remember, you get what you focus on, so focus on being happy, loved, excited, powerful and confident. Imagine that you can choose how you want to feel in any situation. Imagine that you can be in the best possible state for what you want to do. What will you do now? How much better will you feel, and how much more will you get from your social life?

Strong positive feelings can also speed things up and propel you towards your love goal quicker than you can imagine. There is energy in an emotion. If when you imagine the loving, committed relationship you desire, you get excited and enthusiastic about what you see, then you attach a positive emotional charge to it. It is this which speeds thing up and brings it to you. So when you next visualise your wonderful relationship and your perfect partner, really feel the amazing feelings of being totally and completely loved and happy.

Your Practical Magic for Level 3

1. Use the Instant Feel-Good Spell every day for a week. Each day, reinforce the good feelings and notice them getting stronger. Reinforce all your anchors.

2. Before going to any social event, anchor strong feelings of happiness, love, power, excitement, and enthusiasm - any wonderful feelings you can think of.

If you are sure you have completed and cast all your spells for Level 3 you may now precede to Level 4. Good luck

Level 4

Making a Connection – Going Beyond Attraction

Have you ever met someone and instantly warmed to them? Something about them enabled you to get on well right from the start? It wasn't their looks or their money, but something about them attracted you, something you couldn't quite put your finger on. Have you ever known someone who wasn't great looking but attracted other people like a magnet? People wanted to be with that person, be around him or her. That person was always invited out and always the centre of attention. Maybe he or she also had a choice of partners and dates, or maybe this person was already in a loving long-term relationship. They just seem to enchant those around them. Such people aren't special or simply lucky. They attract others because they naturally possess or have cultivated captivating communication skills. They've become good at instantly building and maintaining a connection (or rapport) with everyone they meet. Fortunately, you can learn the magical skill of rapport building that is essential for starting and maintaining an intimate relationship.

Learning how to build rapport quickly and easily brings you a number of benefits.

It makes interacting with people and having relationships much easier. You'll have greater influence in any type of relationship. In fact, how successful you are in achieving the goals you've set yourself will depend on your ability to build rapport with people who can help you on your way. You'll find that the people most willing to help you in any area of your life will be the people you have the most rapport with. If you want to develop a closer relationship with someone you must build and maintain rapport.

Being good at building rapport will also give you more choices in your relationships. You'll be more confident about meeting new people, and you'll find yourself enjoying interacting with greater numbers of people. Increasing your circle of friends and social acquaintances will give you more choices in prospective friends, lovers, or partners.

What exactly is rapport? Psychologists define it as a state in which we *like* one another and feel that we *are like* each other. It's a feeling of closeness and safety and trust and openness. The key to building rapport is to show genuine interest in another person. You can give a person no higher gift than your undivided attention. Doing so will get you noticed. You'll seem different and the person will appreciate you for it.

In this Level you'll learn techniques to help you build rapport quickly with anyone you meet. As you practice and develop these skills your influence will increase in all of your relationships, and you'll be able to build new, mutually respectful, relationships based on trust. You will find yourself enchanting those around you like never before.

How can you instantly appeal to anyone you meet? What magic do you need to build rapport quickly? You've actually been building rapport with people most of your life. Stop for a moment and think about someone whom you had just met and with whom you seemed to hit it off immediately. Think carefully. What was it about that person that made you like him or her? Was it because you had something in common, something that you shared? Maybe you had the similar interests or the same hobbies, or maybe you came from the same part of the world. Maybe you had the same kind of job or career. Maybe you had similar beliefs. Somehow you seemed to be like each other. This perception of likeness is the foundation on which rapport is built. When people think they're like each other, they like each other. The question is, how do you communicate to someone, 'Hi, I'm like you, so you can like me?' to develop a rapport with them?

Psychologists have found that we communicate not only through the words we use, but also through the way we speak and the body language we use. In fact, research has shown that that other people (unconsciously) pay more attention to our body language - the way we stand, our facial expressions, the gestures we use and even the way we breathe - than to what we're actually saying. About fifty five percent of what we communicate is conveyed unconsciously through our body language. Around 38 percent comes from the *way* we speak—the tone of our voice, its volume, its cadence and so on. Only seven percent of what we communicate is conveyed through our actual words.

Like most people, you probably set more store by people's non-verbal behaviour than their words. If a person's words and their body language don't seem to match, you instinctively believe their body language. For example, if someone says, 'What a lovely haircut' with a smirk, their body language (the smirk) will convey the opposite message to your unconscious mind. So you won't believe them. Similarly, if someone says, 'How fascinating' while glancing at her watch, her action will convey that she finds your conversation boring. It's important to watch your body language.

Pay attention to other people's body language too. If you want to build rapport easily and quickly, the most effective means is to match the person's body language first, then their tone of voice, and finally, if you can, the words they use. Here's how.

The Spell of Attraction - How to Attract Using Body Language

The three main ways to build rapport using body language are matching, mirroring and cross-over matching. In matching, you match the other person's body language with your own. For instance, if the other person's right arm was raised and you raised your right arm you'd be matching them. If the person's *left* arm was raised and you raised your *right* arm you'd be creating a mirror image, or *mirroring* them. When you match or mirror another person's body language and behaviour you must be respectful. You must have a genuine desire to get to know the other person and see things from their viewpoint. Be comfortable with yourself when you're matching or mirroring another person. Be natural. Don't match or mirror anything you're uneasy about. Most importantly, have fun!

If it feels more comfortable you can match one aspect of the person's body language with a different part of your body. This technique is called *cross-over matching*. For instance, the famous hypnotherapist Milton Erickson used to match someone's breathing by tapping his finger or his foot.

Here's how to learn the magic of rapport building quickly by matching or mirroring someone's body language.

Posture. Is the person sitting or standing? If he's sitting, what's the angle of his spine? Some people sit with their spines straight; others sit with their spines at an angle. Adopt the same spine angle to develop rapport. Note the relationship between the person's head and shoulders. Does he tip his head to one side? Is his head up? Is it down? Adopting the same relationship between your head and shoulders will also build rapport. Note the person's posture. What's the position of the person's arms in relation to the rest of the body? Are their arms crossed, or by their sides, or does one arm cradle the other elbow? Finally, consider the lower body. What's the position of the legs compared to the rest of the body? Are their legs stretched out in front of them, relaxed, are they crossed, are the knees together, or are their ankles crossed? Match or mirror those positions.

Gestures. What gestures does the person use when he or she talks? You can match and mirror these gestures subtly by using the same or similar gestures when you talk. When you are doing this you must be subtle. Casually, scratch your eyebrow if he scratches his eyebrow, touch your nose if he touches his nose and shrug your shoulders if he shrugs their shoulders. Matching and mirroring somebody's gestures again builds unconscious rapport. Again, always remember that matching must be done with utmost respect and genuine desire to know the other person.

Facial expressions. Note the other person's facial expressions. When he raises his eyebrows raise your eyebrows. When he furrows his brow, furrow yours. When he smiles you smile.

Breathing. Matching breathing is the ultimate way to build rapport with someone. This skill takes some practice. Begin by noticing the rate of the person's breathing and whether the breath originates from the chest or the diaphragm. Here's a tip. When the person is speaking they're breathing out and when they aren't speaking they're breathing in. As long as you breathe out when they're speaking and breathe in when they've stopped you'll be matching their breathing perfectly.

The more often you match and mirror people's body language, the easier and more natural it will become. Adopt a similar posture, gestures and facial expression. Give the same amount of eye contact because that's what the other person is comfortable with. You'll find that you're matching and mirroring unconsciously before long, so just practice and enjoy the results.

How to Make Your Voice Irresistible

Making your voice appealing to others works on the same principle as attracting through body language. You're using the sound of your voice to communicate to someone's unconscious mind: 'Hi, I'm like you, so you can like me'. Using your voice to create rapport is especially useful when you're talking on the telephone. The following spell will make your voice irresistible to anyone.

All you have to do is match the quality of the other person's voice. First, listen out for the pitch and tone of voice. Does the person have a low-pitched voice or a high-pitched voice? Second, note the speed of their speech. Some people speak very slowly, with long pauses in their sentences. Others speak quickly, hardly drawing breath between sentences. Third, pay attention to the timbre or quality of the voice. Some people speak with crystal-clear pronunciation while other people's voices have a distorted, muffled sound. Fourth, notice the volume of the speech. Some people speak quietly while others have loud, booming voices. Fifth, listen for characteristic sounds that accompany the person's speech, such as coughs, hesitations and sighs.

To build rapport, you need to match the tone, tempo, timbre and volume of the person's voice. You may think that being aware of so many details is a lot to think about, and you're right. But fortunately all these factors are connected by the part of the body where the voice originates. Some people speak from right up in their throat. These people will speak rapidly with high-pitched voices; the sound will be clear and loud. Other people speak from their chest; the pitch is a bit lower; they speak a bit more slowly; their voice is a little more resonant and is a bit quieter than most people's. Still other people speak from the pit of their stomach; their speech is quiet, somewhat distorted, low pitched and slow. To match another person's voice, determine where the voice originates. By matching the origin you can match the tone, timbre and tempo of the person's speech. Then match the hesitations and pauses.

Practice as much as you can with various people. You'll eventually match others naturally and unconsciously. You'll notice a difference in the way you get on with people. Communicating what you want will be easy and you'll find that people want to be around you. Don't be surprised if men say they love talking to you and they feel good around you. Men are attracted to women who make them feel good about themselves.

The Magic Words - How to Use Words That Attract

The key principle of attraction is mirroring and matching another person's body language and voice. Matching their words can deepen and complete the attraction. Some people have 'hot' words and phrases that they tend to repeat. For example, you may remember a few years ago teenagers used to say 'awesome' all the time. You might notice your date or the man you are attracted to saying, 'great' or 'absolutely' or 'amazing' frequently. Pick up these words and use them casually in the conversation.

People also have pauses or breaks in their sentences. Some people may say only one or two or three words then pause and then present a few more bits of information before pausing and continuing. Other people may have virtually no breaks at all and put a lot of information into each chunk of speech. They may speak many words before they pause to give you another chunk of information. Again, you can match the pauses and silences in speech, and you can match the size of the person's chunk of information content to further enhance the rapport you have with them.

You can deepen the feeling of closeness and friendship you are developing by mentioning experiences and associations you share with the person. If you have values and beliefs similar to the other person, let him know that. You can also build rapport by respecting and understanding the other person's beliefs and values even if you don't agree with them. Respect for the other person's world view is the foundation of any true relationship. Never ask someone to justify or explain why he or she values something, or believes something to be important. Values aren't logical, and they can't be justified through arguments and rationalisations. If you ask him to explain his values he will feel he is being judged.

Never underestimate the impact you can have on someone through a few carefully chosen words. Amazingly, kind words have been shown to have a positive impact on another's health and well-being.

Saying something kind to someone can feel so wonderful to them. It can comfort them and this comforting feeling can also have a beneficial impact on their health. Your words can trigger positive thoughts, feelings and mental images. The words 'You mean so much to me' or 'I can be myself with you' for instance may mean a lot to the person you say them to and can cause him or her to choose to feel wonderful. This beautiful feeling can have a knock-on effect on their health.

Knowing That You're Successful

How do you know when you've established rapport and the other person is attracted to you? The person might say something like, 'I can't believe that we've only just met', or 'I'm sure I've met you before', or 'I think I know you from somewhere', or 'You really remind me of so and so'. Such statements are attempts to rationalise why they feel attracted to you in such a short time. You yourself may feel a mild sensation of excitement or anticipation. You may experience a pleasant feeling of butterflies in your stomach.

The reason you are learning this magical way to build instant rapport is to enable you to build genuine, interesting, fulfilling relationships with those you meet. If you choose to, you can deepen this connection by noticing the person's good points, what is attractive and worthwhile about them. As you do this, more of these qualities will surface in them when they are around you, and they will feel good about themselves and about you.

So be inspired by others and admire their strengths and good qualities. When you focus on the individual's positive characteristics you are reinforcing the positive beliefs they hold about themselves, and this makes them feel great. Get to know people and remember it is who they are and not what they are, or what they have that matters. Value people for what really matters and they will love you for it.

So when you think about people and when you're with them, focus on their good qualities. Practice and continue to reflect their capabilities and strengths back to them. Doing so will help you see the good in others and develop these qualities in yourself. Your unconscious mind will take your thoughts as a suggestion that you want to be a kind, generous, courageous (or whatever good quality) person too.

Taking Your Charismatic Skills to a New Level

Being good at observing people's body language and tone of voice means that you'll quickly pick up on how they're feeling. Use this technique to help the other person feel relaxed, comfortable and at ease with you. Ask yourself, 'What can I say?

What can I do?' Being generous with your attention will bring you rich rewards.

Although it seems deceptively simple, learn to listen well. People are attracted to those who give them time and attention. Focus on what they're saying. If necessary, repeat it back using their own key words to make them feel that they've been heard.

Practice your new skills on as many people as possible. Widen your social circle so that you're not just interacting with the same people or the same types of people. Deliberately go places where you'll meet people from different backgrounds. Get out there!

What have you always wanted to learn? What have you always wanted to do? What really interests you? Join a class, a club, and a group. Don't think about going to the class or event to meet a partner. If you're a woman don't think that few men will go to what you enjoy. Remember two things: You need only one man, the right man, to be in any one place, and you're going there to be authentically who you are. By nurturing your interests, your self-esteem and your creativity, you'll attract the right person for you.

There are positive, sensitive men with integrity out there, but you will only attract their attention if you give out the right signals. If a man knows his own mind and is self-confident, he will be looking for similar qualities in a mate. He will be looking for someone who is emotionally strong and independent; he is not interested in a love victim. So the best thing you can do is get a life, have fun and then get a man. Men worth having want to be with women they can respect and trust, so nurture these qualities in yourself. Remember that the energy from whatever is going on inside of you will be sent out and reflected back to you in some way.

The Secret to Being Irresistibly Attractive

When you go out to any social occasion, whether it's a business function or a club social, find out in a genuine, respectful way as much as you can about as many people as you can. Go on. Try it.

I'll bet you'll surprise yourself. What's more, I'll bet you'll have a fantastic time.

It is important that you fulfil your own needs and don't expect a man to do that for you. Ask yourself, what makes you happy, what makes you feel good, positive, strong and loved? Coming from a place of strength allows your man to give things freely. Observe what he chooses to give, this will tell you what kind of man he is and whether he is the one for you. Sherry Argov in *Why Men Love Bitches* points out that many women need to receive something from a man that they need to give themselves.

If a woman has a life, interests, friends, work and hobbies then she looks secure and attractive to a man. He knows that he can't drag her away from her life, because she is content with her life, and the more he'll want her. When she is relaxed and casual and treats him just as a friend (if he is truly interested) he is the one who will pursue.

People are also attracted to those who have a genuine interest in others and who feel good about themselves and their lives. These charismatic people have a sense of self-confidence, a kind of inner glow. The key to this, is feeling relaxed and comfortable in your own skin. It is about accepting yourself completely and knowing that you are good enough.

If you make yourself feel comfortable and relaxed, then people you talk to will feel comfortable and relaxed too. So next time you meet someone of the opposite sex, instead of asking yourself 'Am I making a good impression? Will they like me?', ask yourself 'How will knowing this person make me happy?' Interestingly, everyone feels more comfortable around you when you assume you are good enough. Your ease and confidence are deeply attractive. In a social situation you are free to think, 'Who do I want to talk to?' and this makes it all the more interesting.

The thing is you are interesting to others, if you are interested and engaged in the activity or the topic of conversation. What makes us feel good when we flirt is simply enjoying the presence of the other person. People feel good if they believe they are making someone else happy. When you let the person know they are doing that for you, it is a powerful invitation for them to get to know you better.

Maybe you're thinking, 'I'd love to feel like that'. You can if you believe you can. Like everything else in this book, it's simply a question of following instructions and learning the skills of personal transformation. The first and foremost skill in building your self-esteem and confidence is learning to appreciate you and all your good qualities.

The best thing you can do to boost your self-esteem is to recognise the many good things you already have going for you. What are your strengths? What are your good qualities? What are the positive aspects of you? What do you like about yourself? Many of us at first may not feel that we have any or very little. But believe me, that's not true. Every single one of us has positive traits and gifts, even if you haven't recognised them yet. You owe it to yourself to discover yours. Think about all the positives in your life - your abilities, your accomplishments. Think about all the people who like you, the people who look up to you and respect you.

As you begin to focus on what is good about you, the law of attraction will show you even more things that are terrific about you. You must shift your attention and start to think about all the things that you really like about you. Look out for the positives in you. As you concentrate more and more on those things, the universe will show you a multitude of marvellous things about you. All you have to do is to take one thought of something good about you, keep focussing on it, and the law of attraction will respond by giving you more similar thoughts.

Here's the Instant Confidence Booster to help you on your way. Use this confidence booster any time, but especially before you attend any social function. Enjoy yourself!

Instant Confidence Booster

What makes you feel terrific about being you? What are your best qualities? Sit down and complete the following statements.

My best quality is

_____

I feel powerful when

_____

My greatest strengths are

_____

I'm most proud of

_____

I feel strong when

_____

I'm at my happiest when

_____

My greatest asset is

_____

I feel attractive when

_____

I feel sexy when

_____

I feel excited when

_____

I'm at my best when

_____

I'm most confident when

_____

Women who are confident and know their worth have a special air about them. Around men they are relaxed and don't appear to care that much. This makes them irresistible to the opposite sex.

Putting your life, values and priorities first shows that you are confident and have high self-esteem. It tells a man how much you value yourself and your life. Furthermore, it gives him a clear message on how you expect to be treated. Who do you think is more attractive to men and happy in herself, the nice girl or the Goddess?

The nice girl lets slide what she used to value and what used to be important in her life.

The Goddess prioritises her preferences, values and the things that matter to her.

When her guy's in a good mood the nice girl feels good; when he snubs her, she feels bad.

The Goddess is more balanced and confident. This means that someone else's mood doesn't have too much impact on her. She does something that makes her happy, such as seeing friends or going to the spa.

The nice girl often gives too much emotionally first, and then tries to get him to return the favours later.

The Goddess waits and sees. She takes her time and gives emotionally only when she knows it is reciprocal. The Goddess takes care of herself. She matters, she is important.

Now complete the following exercise to make you feel even more confident and good about yourself. Read the instructions through first before doing the exercise.

A Double Shot of Confidence

1.   Now that you're feeling great, remember a time when you felt especially confident. Don't think this has to be when you were an adult. You can go back to a childhood memory to a time when you felt really good about your self. Perhaps someone praised you or you did something you were really proud of. One of my clients recalled the first time she tied her shoe laces! Go back to that time now. See what you saw, hear what you heard and feel how you felt. Double the feelings of confidence, treble them. Feel them strongly in your whole body. Move them around your body.

2.   Now squeeze together your thumb and the middle finger of you right hand. Make sure you are feeling those wonderful strong confident feelings as you squeeze your fingers together.

3.   Press firmly until the feeling begins to subside.

4.   Repeat steps 1 to 3 until simply squeezing the fingers together will bring up these feelings of terrific self-confidence.

5.   Keep squeezing the thumb and middle finger together and

think about a situation in which you want to feel confident. Imagine things going exactly the way you want them. See what you'll see, hear what you'll hear and feel how great you'll feel.

Great! Simply notice how much more positive and confident you feel after using this technique. Practice this simple technique every day for just one week and notice how much more confident and happier you feel.

Thinking positively and identifying your positive characteristics are the two most effective ways to improve your self-image. And as your self-respect and self-confidence grows, others will follow your lead and accept and respect you too.

You are beginning to realise that improving your self-image is easy and simple. Accepting yourself is one of the most important things you can do to feel relaxed with others, and for them to feel relaxed with you. Because you accept yourself, the law of attraction dictates that you will project this out and on to others. Thus they will not only accept you but feel accepted too. When you express a self-accepting demeanour it helps others to follow your lead and feel calm and relaxed with you. This is a very powerful reason for being accepting of yourself when you're around others.

Unless you love yourself, it's hard for you to believe that anyone else will. Self-esteem is important for a healthy relationship. When you truly like yourself, in spite of any weaknesses and failings you may think you have, you'll feel confident. And when you feel confident and secure within yourself, you can relax and just enjoy being with your partner for the happiness they bring to your life, not because you feel you need them to survive.

As well as accepting yourself and improving your self-confidence, it is also important for you to know when you feel loved, what it is that makes you feel loved, whether you are in a relationship or not. This helps you to understand yourself and your needs better. When you are next in relationship you will be able to succinctly tell your partner what makes you feel loved and you will know what to do for yourself so that you feel valued.

As a start, do the following exercise.

Feeling loved and valued

Step 1. Take a sheet of paper and write: 'As a child, I felt loved when...' Next, write down as many things as you can that made you feel loved. Your list may include what a parent or carer said. You might remember physical affection such as cuddles. You may remember the time they spent with you, or presents bought. Or perhaps it was someone cooking your favourite food or coming with you on your paper round for you.

Step 2. On a second sheet of paper write: 'I feel loved when...' and write down all the things you can think of that your current or previous partner(s) have done that make you feel loved.

Step 3. Have a look at the list and think about which things you prefer. Next time you find you're not feeling loved and valued, remember what you've written and ask your partner to show their love in a way that's more meaningful to you.

Energise Your Love Life

People who are excited about their own lives, full of energy and enthusiasm, will attract the attention of others. But even these people don't feel energetic and enthusiastic all the time. They too need strategies and techniques to motivate and energise themselves. The strategies you're learning in this book are doing exactly the same thing for you. Before I end this Level, let me share one more simple, yet effective, way to energise yourself.

The Breath of Life Force

1. Sit comfortably with your hands resting on your lap. Have your spine straight and allow your shoulders to relax. Take a deep breath through your nose, filling up your lungs.
2. Breathe out through your mouth, making a 'haa' sound. Continue breathing in this way for ten minutes. If time allows do

your 'haa' breathing for fifteen minutes.
3. Notice how energised and full of life you feel.
Just Go for It
What if you could use rapport to build relationships easily and effortlessly? What if you knew the secret of charisma? Imagine how much more fun having a relationship will be and how much easier it is to interact with people. Just suppose you have greater influence in any relationship and you can create supportive, nourishing, respectful relationships based on trust. What kind of life would you now create for yourself? What kind of relationships will you have? How much happier and more fulfilled will you be? What will you go for?

Your Practical Magic for Level 4

1. For the rest of the week watch people in cafes, shops, restaurants and other places where people gather to socialise. Observe people who are in rapport and people who aren't in rapport.
2. Practice mirroring and matching the body language of people you come into contact with this week. Match their posture, their gestures, and their facial expressions, even their breathing. Note what happens.
3. When you have a conversation with someone this week show genuine interest in what that person is saying. Imagine they have great knowledge and wisdom. Notice their assets and strengths.
4. Use your *confidence booster* and give yourself a *double shot of confidence* before you go out to any social events from now on.
You may now move on to Level 5.

Level 5

Use the Powerful Magic of Beliefs – To Change Your Life

The law of attraction states that like attracts like. So we are just like magnets, attracting situations and people that match the energy we are sending out into the world. We can attract negative, fearful, angry or sad situations and people, if we send out negative energy such as anger, fear or sadness. Conversely, we can attract positive situations and people, if we send out positive energy such as happy and joyful thoughts. We are attracting all of the time, but sometimes we attract things that we don't really want. So what could be getting in the way of you attracting what you want into your life?

The beliefs you hold about yourself and what you believe you deserve in life may be getting in the way of attracting the kind of loving relationship you want. Don't underestimate the power of beliefs. Your beliefs about yourself have determined your life so far, and changing your beliefs about yourself, other people and relationships will change your life. Your beliefs either allow you to achieve what you want in life, or they act as barriers to stop you getting what you want. They act like self-fulfilling prophecies. For example, if you believe you're not attractive you'll unconsciously act in ways that put other people off and, in so doing, you'll confirm your belief. In contrast, if you believe you're attractive you'll unconsciously act in an open and confident way, and people's warmth towards you will reinforce your belief. What you choose to believe about yourself and others is the most powerful thing you can do to shape your world and your relationships. What you believe influences every area of your life, from your relationships to your intelligence, from career choices to happiness.

Beliefs are like putting on special spectacles to look at the world. If the lenses are covered with pessimistic beliefs, such as mistrust, you'll see the world as full of untrustworthy people who betray you. In contrast, if you coat your lenses with constructive beliefs, such as people are friendly and kind or I can trust myself, your world will be friendly, sociable and fun, where you'll make good choices.

Your beliefs aren't facts; they aren't objective truths. They're simply your way of looking at the world based on your individual experiences. Your beliefs come from events in your childhood, from your family, school, and work, and from genetic influences. These combinations give you your unique model of the world. This model tells you how things are supposed to work, how people are supposed to behave, what's supposed to happen in relationships, what's possible to achieve. In other words, this model gives your beliefs about yourself, about other people and relationships, about what you're capable of doing.

Your beliefs are powerful magic: they have a far greater influence on what you do than so-called objective truths. A graphic illustration of the power of beliefs comes from the world of athletics. Before 1954, no one believed that a human being could run a mile in less than four minutes and so no one did. Then Roger Bannister broke the four-minute mile barrier. As if by magic, it was like a spell had been lifted. Slowly, other athletes began running a mile in less than four minutes and now that feat has become relatively commonplace among top athletes. Once people believed it was possible (the spell was lifted) it became possible. Roger Bannister changed athletes' beliefs about what was possible and therefore changed what they were capable of doing.

Similarly, in the nineteenth century passengers refused to travel on the earliest steam trains because they believed that going at the phenomenal speed of thirty miles per hour would kill them. The train inventors and innovators had to go on the trains themselves to break the spell (the belief) and prove that travelling at such speeds was safe. Now, of course, we get on trains without thinking and travel at speeds of up to six hundred miles per hour on airplanes.

Your beliefs influence all your decisions, how you feel about events, whether you achieve the goals you set and, ultimately, the direction you go in life. So what sort of belief spells have you been casting unwarily over your life and what can you do about it?

The changes that matter most are often not the changes in the world around us but changes in our own perception. Marcel Proust once said, 'The real voyage of discovery consists not in seeking new lands, but in seeing with different eyes'. What is more, we can change the way we perceive in an instant. Sometimes even the smallest change in what you believe can make a huge difference to your life.

How to Identify Problem Belief Spells (Limiting Beliefs)

What can you do if you think that your beliefs may be stopping you from having the relationship you want and are limiting you? At this stage you may not be consciously aware of your beliefs. Yet, you project these beliefs out onto the world so that everything around you is a manifestation of your deeply held unconscious beliefs. So first, you must identify these beliefs. To begin to understand your beliefs and how they affect your life, consider the following questions:

- How do you feel about your life?
- Do you feel confident and happy?
- Do you feel in control?
- Do you feel you have the power to shape your life? Or do you feel that others have power over you?
- Do you feel cared for, loved and supported?

If you answered 'no' to any of these questions, your beliefs may be preventing you from getting what you want. Don't worry. In this Level and the following Levels, I'll give you the psychological techniques (or counter spells) that will help you to get rid of these self-defeating beliefs and instil new, empowering, beliefs instead.

Recall the goal you set for your relationship in Level 2. To reach your desired destination, you need to believe three things about this goal:

- That it's *possible* to achieve it.
- *You can* achieve it.
- You *deserve* to achieve it.

Bring your relationship goal to mind and think: 'This goal is possible.' 'I can achieve this goal'. 'I deserve to achieve this goal.'

Notice any uncomfortable feelings that suggest you may have self-doubts and limiting beliefs about yourself. Call to mind any likely beliefs that might be obstacles to your success. Say to yourself, 'I will not achieve this relationship goal because...' and list all the reasons that come to mind. List your beliefs about yourself or other people. Good. You've identified the obstacles (the problem belief spells) to your success. Fortunately, I can give you three powerful tools from my magic kit to change your self-defeating beliefs into empowering ones.

How to Cast New Empowering Belief Spells

The magic of Neuro Linguistic Programming (NLP) and ancient Hawaiian Huna provides a whole range of simple psychological techniques to change beliefs that no longer work and are holding you back. I'll start by giving you some simple spells that will help you to take a new perspective on any experience in your past. The next Levels will take your skills and understanding to an advanced level of psycho-spell dynamics. Be sure to read and practice the following techniques carefully.

The Belief Transformer Spell

NLP shows that what you believe and feel about a certain experience depends on the meaning you give it. That meaning is dependent on the sequence of the *internal representations* of the experience that you hold in your head. For instance, when you think of the experience a picture may come to mind (this is a visual representation). You may also recall certain sounds (this is called an audio representation). You may associate certain physical sensations and feelings with the experience, such as butterflies in your stomach or a sinking feeling (this is termed a kinaesthetic representation).

Simply changing the sequence of your internal representations (images, sounds, feelings and sensations) can change the meaning that the particular experience or event has for you, which in turn allows you to change your beliefs about it. It's that easy. The Belief Transformer Spell is a very effective method of changing unhelpful beliefs into empowering ones.

Begin by identifying a belief that you wish you didn't have. For example, 'I don't deserve a loving relationship', or 'I'm not good enough' or whatever the unhelpful belief is. Then answer the questions in the grid as quickly as possible. Write your answers in column 1. *Don't* pause to think about the questions. Just write the first thing that pops into your head. For example, if you believe 'I'm not attractive' note the first picture that pops into your head as you think about that belief. This picture could be in colour or black and white; it could be close up or distant; it could be a moving picture or still, like a photograph; it could be bright or dim. These qualities of the picture are called sub-modalities. The founders of NLP, Richard Bandler and John Grinder, discovered that simply changing these qualities or sub-modalities can change the meaning of the belief or event, and how you feel about it. If you change them significantly the belief will no longer be true for you.

So here's how you do it in three easy stages. First, you're given a way of dispelling your old self-defeating belief. Next, you're asked for an empowering belief you'd like to have instead. Finally, you're shown how to instil this desirable new belief.

Once again, read through the procedure carefully and then proceed with this transformative spell.

Step One: Vanish Your Limiting Belief
Do you have a belief that you wish you didn't have? What is it? As you think about that belief, do you have a picture? (Take the first image that pops into your mind.) It's essential that you go through the following *quickly*. Put your answers in the first column.

Do you have a picture? Is it?	1	2
Sub-modalities (Qualities)		
Black & white or colour? Near or far? Bright or dim? Large, medium or small? Are you looking through your own eyes (associated) Or do you see yourself in the picture (dissociated)? Focused or unfocused? Focus changing or steady? Picture framed or panoramic? Movie or still? Amount of contrast? Three-D or flat? What is angle viewed from?		
Are any sounds important? If yes, what are they?		
Location? Direction?		

Inside you or outside? Loud or soft? Fast or slow? Pitch - high or low? Distinct quality of sound (Timbre)? Pauses? Rhythm or tempo of sound (Cadence)? Duration?		
Are there any feelings that are important? If yes, what are they?		
Location? Size? Shape? Intensity? Steady or not? Movement? Duration? Vibration? Pressure? Weight?		

1. Okay, good, now put that picture to the side. Now do you have a belief that's no longer true, for example, the belief that Santa Claus is real or you are 5 years old? Good, what is it? You need a ridiculous belief that is no longer true for you (state this ridiculous belief in the present tense, e.g. 'I am 5 years old', 'I believe in Santa Claus). As you think about this old belief do you have a picture? Take the first picture that pops into your mind.

2. Do exactly the same as you did for you first picture: quickly go through the questions in the table above and put your answers in column 2.

3. Now bringing up the picture of the unwanted belief, change the sub-modalities (qualities of the images, sounds and feelings) of the unwanted belief (first picture) into the sub modalities of the belief that is no longer true. For example, if your picture of Santa

Claus was bright, in colour, and you were looking down at it, do the same for the first picture you associated with your limiting belief. That is, make that image brighter, in colour and look down at the same angle at it.

4. What do you think about your old negative limiting belief now?

Step 2: Identify a New Empowering Belief
What would you like to believe instead of that old belief you used to have? For example, 'I deserve a loving, supportive, relationship'. 'I am love'.

Step 3: Instil the New Desirable Belief
1. Do you have a different belief that for you is absolutely definitely true, for example, that the sun will come up tomorrow, or that it's good to breathe. Good, what is it? As you think about that belief do you see a picture? (The first thing that pops into your head.)
2. Again run quickly through sub-modalities (qualities of the image) and put your answers in column 1.

Do you have a picture? Is it?	1	2
Are any sounds important? If yes, what are they?		
Location of sound? Direction? Inside you or outside? Loud or soft? Fast or slow? Pitch - high or low? Distinct quality of sound (Timbre)? Pauses? Rhythm or tempo of		

sound (Cadence)? Duration		
Are any feelings important? If yes, what are they?		
Location? Size? Shape? Intensity? Steady or not? Movement? Duration? Vibration? Pressure? Weight?		

3. Now call to mind what you would like to believe instead of that old belief: 'I can have a loving relationship', 'I deserve to be loved and appreciated'. Whatever belief that is great for you. As you think of this new belief, do you have a picture?

4. Now look at column 1 and notice the sub-modalities or qualities for the belief that is absolutely true (sun will come up or it's good to breathe). Change the sub modalities of the new empowering belief ('I deserve to be loved' and so on) into the sub modalities of the belief that is absolutely true.

5. Now what do you believe? Why do you believe you have this new belief?

Use this technique to rid yourself of any beliefs that are holding you back from getting what you want and to instil empowering, motivating, beliefs that will help you to achieve the love goals you've set. Go for it!

The Spell of Reframes – the art of generating a positive perspective

Another powerful technique for changing the meaning of any experience, and thereby changing how you feel and what you believe about it, is the reframing spell. The reframing spell involves changing how you see a particular event or experience in your life, so that you see it in a more positive light.

I have noticed that people who overcome problems or find solutions to them, rarely see what happens to them as a disaster or tragedy, instead they reframe it as a challenge. What other people may regard a as a terrible event, they see as an opportunity. This is something we can all do. We just have to look at a situation in a different way, and put the incident into a more positive context. It is about having a point of view that is beneficial to us. What determines the outcome is not only what happens to us, but how we interpret it.

The reframing spell helps you to change the meaning of a painful experience. You can use this technique anywhere and in any situation.

It works on the principle that the meaning we give to behaviour depends on the context in which the behaviour takes place. Let me give you a simple example. Suppose I said that I saw a woman slowly undressing a man for bed. If we know that these two are lovers, we might think, 'How sexy'. However, in a different context - say, that of a hospital - it's a nurse going about her duties. It's the same behaviour (undressing) in a different context, so it has a different meaning.

Reframing lets you change the meaning of an event or behaviour by seeing it in a different way. There are two ways to use a reframing spell, you can reframe or change the context of the behaviour or reframe its meaning.

A *context reframe* changes the context of the behaviour to give it a more constructive meaning. For example, when I think about my past relationships I might think, 'I'm so stubborn', and 'I'm too head-strong'. If I stop to reframe that behaviour I might think, 'Yes, but that's been useful when I've had to argue a point to get my clients what they want'. So, in a different context the behaviour becomes an advantage. Similarly, you may think, 'I think I'm too sensitive'. Your reframe spell could be, 'It's good to be in touch with my feelings. That will really help me be aware of how other people feel. It's good to be aware of my family or my friends' needs. That has made me a good friend'.

In fact you can help friends or family members by reframing any negative beliefs they have about themselves. If a friend says to you, 'Sometimes I feel I'm not in control', your reframe for her could be, 'It's good that you're not in control all the time because that means you can go with the flow. Isn't it good to relax sometimes, and just let things happen'. So in other contexts, all these 'problems' are turned into strengths.

A *meaning reframe* spell involves asking yourself what else a behaviour or event could mean. The meaning reframe helps to change a negative perception of an event or behaviour to a positive one. For example, if my friend complains that her married friends no longer ask her out, I could respond, 'Well, that's a great opportunity to go out and meet new people and have fun with single friends. I bet that's much more fun!' Or, say, a colleague at work says, 'My car broke down yesterday'. I could respond, 'I'll bet that gave you a good opportunity to walk and get all that exercise you've been meaning to get'.

A meaning reframe is also useful when you feel that your reaction to an event or situation was over emotional or a mistake. For instance, if my friend complained, 'I feel upset when no one calls me', I could reply, 'You like being in company and people like being with you. You're a sociable person'. Or if your friend says, 'I get angry waiting for people to arrive'. You could respond, 'You're concerned about being on time because you have a lot respect for others and yourself.'

Whether you use a context reframe or a meaning reframe, you're asking yourself, 'What else could this experience mean?' 'What would I like it to mean?' Reframing lets you see things in a different, more constructive light; it also gives you more choice about how you will respond to a particular event.

The more skilful you become at the art of reframing, the more choices you give yourself in life. Having more choices means you will be more flexible in the way you respond to situations. Flexibility is what gives you power and self-control in your life.

The metaphor of the branch of a tree makes this clear. During a storm the branch which is more pliable is likely to bend in the wind and remain undamaged, whereas one that is rigid is more likely to snap and break off.

The 'Crafting' of Questions

This third spell from NLP uses carefully crafted questions to magically change your beliefs by changing the meaning of an event or behaviour. You'll remember from Level 1 that consciously you're aware of only around seven separate pieces of information at any given time. Yet you're bombarded with information from all directions, and over your lifetime you'll have had millions of experiences and processed millions of pieces of information. Your unconscious mind contains all the thoughts, feelings, sensations, resources, possibilities, beliefs and values that you're not paying attention to at this moment. It's also the repository of all our memories, everything that you've experienced, everything that has happened to you.

For the conscious mind to handle the millions of pieces of information held by your unconscious mind, it has to minimise them by *distorting*, *generalising* and *deleting* your actual experiences. It is as if there is a spell cast around you, which affects the way you see the world. So what you see and experience is not what is really happening in its entirety but your own biased version of it. Let me explain this in more detail.

All the information that comes into your mind through your senses (sight, sound, smells, tastes and touches) is filtered so that your conscious mind can handle it. This filtering process distorts, generalises and deletes the total experience. *Distorting* your experiences changes them in some way. You can exaggerate an experience, embellish it, make it bigger, 'and blow it out of proportion'; you can add things that were not there.

If you've ever noticed someone coming towards you in a quiet street and thought he looked a bit shady, but when he got nearer he looked perfectly nice and normal, you've experienced distortion. Or if you've noticed something small and dark on the floor through the corner of your eye and thought it was a spider, when it was only a lump of hair, then again you have experienced distortion. Or maybe you plan to meet your new boyfriend after work for a drink. You're a bit late and your boyfriend looks annoyed and preoccupied as you sit down. He doesn't ring you over the next four days and you assume that he's doing it to punish you or no longer wants to see you. Again you've distorted your experience in many ways: by assuming that your boyfriend was annoyed because of your lateness, by assuming that his not calling was to punish you, and by assuming that his lack of contact for several days means he no longer wants to see you.

When we distort we often jump to conclusions, assuming that people have particular motives with little evidence. What is more, there is now compelling evidence that men and women think differently and therefore may ascribe completely different meanings to the same situation. This is worth bearing in mind the next time you jump to conclusions regarding a man's behaviour.

Women and men are different in a number of ways. And yes, it's official, women *do* talk more than men. Women on average speak 23,000 words a day while men speak 12,000. Of course, there will be some exceptions to this rule. We all know some men who could talk for their country.

Further studies also show that women are also more adept at using both sides of their brains simultaneously. This means women can talk about their feelings as they feel them. They can feel an emotion and talk at the same time. While this comes naturally to a woman, men find this difficult to do. Instead of talking about his feelings, a man may channel his emotions into actions – he may cut the grass, paint the living room, go out with his mates, write that report, want to have sex and so on. It's important not to hastily jump to conclusions about what he is feeling and thinking. If he doesn't talk with you right away about his feelings, or he goes out with his mates for the evening, this does not mean that he doesn't want to communicate his feelings.

The next mistake we can make is to take one event and

generalise it so that it represents a whole group or class of experiences. *Generalisation* is where you generate conclusions from that single example. For instance, as a child you saw how your parents treated each other and you took that behaviour as a model of how couples live together. Unconsciously, you may come to believe that every couple fights and argues or jealousy is a demonstration of love. Your beliefs are generalisations about how the world works and how relationships work - or don't work - based on what you've experienced. Your beliefs help you to predict what may happen in the future. Because you take them to be absolutely true you pay attention to instances that confirm them, but you often ignore or discount experiences that challenge them. This attitude is fine for beliefs that empower you but not so good for beliefs that make you feel bad.

Deleting leaves out some parts of your experiences because you don't have the words to express them, or you think them unimportant or you didn't notice them at the time. For example, a man watching his favourite football team on television didn't hear the telephone ringing, or a woman didn't see a junior work colleague while she was talking with senior executives from a company she hoped to do business with. In terms of relationships we might not see all the small things our partner does for us, such as tidying after us, making us a cup of tea or listening to our complaints about work or family.

In summary, your conscious mind distorts, generalises and deletes information to give you a selective view of reality resulting in your model of the world. In other words, your conscious mind has cast a spell of enchantment around you. This enchantment, or selective model, may be holding you back and preventing you from having the relationship you want.

So how can you break the enchantment, change your beliefs and give yourself more choice? Well, asking the magic questions is one of the most powerful ways to alter your thinking. 'The Magic Questions – Breaking the Enchantment' was developed from John Grinder and Richard Bandler's *The Meta-Model*. It is a series of questions designed to help you to recognise how you have enchanted yourself, that is, how you distort, generalise and delete your experiences. It will help you to discover any hidden disempowering, de-motivating beliefs that may be sustaining difficulties in your relationships. It will also help you to choose more empowering beliefs that will transform how you relate to others and your intimate relationships.

In the following table are three columns. The first column contains everyday examples of enchantments, that is, how your mind distorts, generalises or deletes information. The second column contains the magic questions you can ask to break the enchantment and give yourself more choice about how you see the world. By uncovering information, clarifying meaning and bringing to light any self-defeating beliefs hidden in your unconscious mind, these questions will help you to become aware of the root cause of any problems you're experiencing in your relationships.

Use the Magic Questions to recognise the patterns you use in your internal dialogue. Be aware of how you're creating your internal world. As you become familiar with the Magic Questions you'll use them in your everyday life. They are amazingly useful tools for giving you the power to shape your reality.

Breaking Enchantments - The Magic Questions

The Self-Imposed Enchantments	Magic Questions	How the Questions Break Enchantments – See More Clearly
Distortions: Information is distorted in a way that limits choice and leads to unnecessary problems and pain in:		
1. Mind Reading: Thinking that you know another person's internal state. Projecting your internal map of the world onto that person's mind. Example: 'He doesn't like me'.	'How do you know he doesn't like you?'	Recovers the source of the information.

2. Judgments: Opinions stated as if they were facts. The person doing the judging is missing, and often the standard by which the judgment is being made is also left out. Examples: a) 'It's bad to be dependent on others'. b) 'She's too sensitive'	'Who says it's bad?' 'According to whom?' 'How do you know it's bad?' 'Who says?' 'According to whom?' 'How do you know she's too sensitive?'	Gathers evidence. Recovers the source of the belief.
3. Cause/Effect: Thinking which implies that another person's behaviour can 'make' another person respond in a particular way because the behaviour 'causes' the response. Example: 'You make me sad'.	'How does what I'm doing cause you to choose to feel sad?' or 'How, specifically?'	Recovers the choice.
4. Complex Equivalence: Two statements interpreted as meaning the same thing. Examples: 'He's always late (therefore) he doesn't care'. 'She isn't looking at me (therefore) she's not listening to what I'm saying'.	'How does his being late mean that he doesn't care?' 'Have you ever been late and cared about someone?' 'Have you ever not looked at someone and listened to what they were saying?' 'Have there been times when this wasn't true?'	Recovers exact meaning. Offers counter-example.
5. Universals: Words like 'every', 'all', 'never', 'everyone', and 'nobody'. Something that may be true in one context is applied to every context. Examples: 'She *never* listens to me'. 'He *always* does that'.	Find counter-examples. 'Never?' 'What would happen if she did?' 'Always?' 'What would happen if he	Recovers counter-examples. effects, and outcomes.

	didn't?'	
6a. Modal Operators of Possibility: Words that define what's possible, as in 'can', 'can't', 'will', 'won't', 'may', 'may not', 'possible', 'impossible'. Example: 'I *can't* tell him the truth'.	a. 'What prevents you?' 'What would happen if you did?'	Recovers causes.
b. Modal Operators of Necessity: Words that set rules are necessary and appropriate. As in 'should', 'shouldn't', 'must', 'must not', 'have to', 'need to', 'necessary'. Example: 'I *must* talk to her'.	b. 'What would happen if you did?' 'What would happen if you didn't?'	Recovers effects or outcomes.
7. Nominalisations: Verbs turned into abstract nouns. Examples: 'It won't work'. 'The *stress* is too much for me', 'Our relationship isn't working'.	'How could believing that contribute to it not working?' 'How are you being stressed?' 'How are you stressing yourself?' 'What is it about the way you're relating that's causing trouble?'	Turns it back into a process, recovers specifics.
8. Unspecified verb deletes exactly how the event happened. Example: 'He rejected me'.	'How, specifically?'	Uncovers how the event happened.
9. Simple Deletions: Something important missed out of the sentence: Example: 'I'm uncomfortable'.	a. 'About what or whom?'	Recovers deletion.
b. Lack of Referential Index (missing persons): Unspecified person or thing taking the action or being affected by the action. Example: 'Nobody listen to me'.	b. 'Who, specifically, doesn't listen to you?'	Recovers referential index (missing person or thing).
c. Comparative Deletions: comparing one thing with another but leaving out the basis for comparison, as in 'better', 'best',	c. 'Better than whom?' 'Better at what?' 'Compared with whom or	Recovers basis for comparison.

'worse', 'worst', 'more', 'less', 'most', 'least'. Example: 'She's a better person'.	what?'	

Believe and Succeed

What if you could identity all the beliefs that are holding you back? What if you could change your beliefs about yourself, about others and about relationships? What if you could choose to believe whatever you wanted to believe? What would you choose? What do you want to believe instead? Imagine having constructive, empowering beliefs about yourself and what you're capable of. Imagine creating a new life because of what you now believe. What you choose to believe will influence all the decisions you make from now on. Those decisions will help you to achieve the goals you've set for your relationship.

Your Practical Magic for Level 5

1. Use the Belief Transformer to dispel any self-defeating beliefs that are holding you back. Replace them with empowering, motivating beliefs about yourself and relationships.
2. Notice any situation that you feel uncomfortable about this week. Maybe you feel unhappy about your own behaviour or your response to someone else's behaviour. Use the reframing spells to see your behaviour from a new perspective.
3. If you feel bad about something this week, use the appropriate 'Breaking the Enchantment – Magic Questions' to find out what's behind your feelings.
4. Think of a belief that you want to be true and 'act as if' it is true all week.

You are doing great. When you have completed all your tasks for Level 5, now move on to Level 6.

Level 6

The Spell of Self-Transformation – The Swan Emerges

In order to feel that you are deeply attractive to another human being, you must firstly feel happy and attractive in yourself. To achieve your goal of attracting your future spouse (or long-term partner), it is important to have a sense of inner well-being. How do you feel about your body and the way you look? Are you happy with your weight and body shape? Do you feel healthy and fit? Do you feel you have enough energy? Do you feel calm and peaceful most of the time?

Rhonda Byrne in *The Secret* tells us that our thoughts give out vibrations and energy, and the more positive the thought the higher frequency. When we begin to treat ourselves with love and respect, we get on to a higher frequency and emit a powerful positive signal to the universe. The universe through the law of attraction then populates your life with people who love and respect you. So the work you do is always on you. You are responsible for your own happiness and peace of mind.

You need to nurture and develop yourself first so that you have something to give to the people in your world. When you make your joy and happiness a priority, then this high frequency you are on will radiate and touch everyone around you. When you make your happiness top of the agenda and do what makes you feel good, you are great to be around and you are a wonderful example to everyone who knows you.

This Level is about maximising your health, fitness and emotional well-being to be the best you can be.

Being as healthy as you can be (even if you have a chronic condition or disability) is essential if you are to live your life to the full and achieve what you really want. Maximising your health gives you the vitality and energy you need to create and maintain a loving, committed relationship. To feel attractive to others you first need to feel happy with your body. To feel loved by others you must first love and cherish you.

When you feel bad about yourself you are sucking the energy and life out of you. This happens because everything that is life giving and beneficial for you on every level, including health, wealth and love, is on the highest frequency of joy and feeling good. The feeling of wellness and health and having a boundless supply of energy are all on the frequency of happiness and joy. When you don't feel good about yourself, and you look for the negatives about you, you are on the frequency that will attract people that will criticise you, and situations, and circumstances that will continue to make you feel bad about you.

The importance of the 'Bodymind'

So what is health anyway and how can you optimise yours? Well, we need to recognise that there is no division between the mind and the body, they are in fact one entity. Our mind and emotions are present everywhere in our body. The body and mind should really be termed the 'bodymind'. We have known for many years now that our thoughts and feelings directly affect the functioning of our body. A very simple example of this is when we cry. It is our thoughts, which lead to sad feelings, which cause our body to produce the tears that trickle down our cheeks. Similarly, happy thoughts trigger happy feelings that may, if strong enough, result in the physical reaction of a belly laugh. These reactions are all simple ways in which your thoughts directly influence your body.

Many biological scientists, psychologists and psychotherapists now agree that the mind (conscious and unconscious) influences and is present in the form of 'intelligence' throughout the entire body. Every feeling and every thought you have sends tiny messages out to your body. Our bodies are so sensitive to our emotions that strong negative emotions such as anger or stress can actually produce physical symptoms. For example, although heart disease can have many causes, stress is recognised as a leading factor. Similarly, stress is implicated in a wide range of physical illnesses, including asthma, certain cancers and stroke.

If an individual has cancer then denying or suppressing a strong negative emotion like anger, sadness or stress it can actually accelerate the progression of this disease (Gross 1989). Research shows that cancers progress faster in people who hold on to deep emotional pain over many years. However, the good news is that by releasing emotional pain the person can slow down the progression of disease and help the body to embark on its healing process.

Researchers have also found that when we express our thoughts, feelings and traumas, by talking about them or writing them down, our immune systems grow stronger.

Dr. David Hamilton in his fascinating book *It's the Thought that Counts* tells us about an important scientific study which showed how our thinking can affect our immune system. An American research team in 1995 asked one group of participants to think about 'care and compassion' (positive emotions) and another group to think about 'anger and frustration' (negative emotions). The scientists then measured the immune responses of each group. The astonished researchers found that thinking about care and compassion strengthened the immune system compared with frustration and anger.The evidence suggests that being caring and compassionate is not only good for our relationships but also for our bodies!

Although we are not consciously aware of it, we are curing ourselves of many aches, pains and illnesses all of the time. Doctors now recognise the power of belief to heal many minor (and major) ailments. They know that people can heal themselves if they believe in the treatment they're receiving, even if it has no active effective ingredients. This psychological reaction, called the placebo effect, shows the power of belief in the healing process.

I heard a wonderful example of this at a 'Mind Body Soul'

Fayre in Dundee, Scotland. The speaker, Dr David Hamilton, who trained as an organic chemist, told us about clinical trials examining the effectiveness of aspirin in treating headaches. He explained how scientific research has consistently found one particular brand of aspirin to be the most effective in treating common headaches. This aspirin had the same chemical properties as the other aspirins, the only difference was that it had a red cross painted on it. Essentially, it was patients' beliefs about what the symbol (red cross) represented that increased the effectiveness of the aspirin. What we believe is a powerful factor in enabling us to ameliorate or even cure certain bodily symptoms.

Other investigations into the placebo effect suggest that in some circumstances the mind can actually overrule the body. In *Destiny vs Freewill*, Dr David Hamilton explains how beliefs can cause allergic reactions in the absence of an allergen, and prevent allergic reactions in the presence of an allergen among susceptible individuals. In this study, the researchers took one group of students who were known to be allergic to poison ivy, blindfolded them and rubbed them with a leaf. The scientists told them it was poison ivy and as a result they came out in a rash. However, the leaf was only a maple leaf! It was simply their belief that caused the rash. The researchers told the other group they were being rubbed with a maple leaf but it actually was poison ivy. The second group did not come out in a rash. Their belief had overruled their typical allergic reaction to poison ivy.

Using your imagination and visualising healing in your body can bring about actual physical healing. There is a wonderfully inspiring story in the book *Creating Miracles* by Carolyn Miller, about a patient suffering severe liver damage resulting from an illness, who used visualisation to great effect. The man was told he would have to live the rest of his life hooked up to a machine to maintain his liver. However, he had read about visualisation and decided to imagine having a healthy liver. In the next few months he spent hours visualising using a toothbrush to clean his liver one cell at a time. At the beginning he saw his liver as a black lump but, as he patiently imagined cleaning it, he eventually could envisage his liver as healthy and pink.

A few months later he had an accident at home in which all his tubes were ripped out. He was rushed to hospital for an emergency operation. When the doctors X-rayed him they were amazed to discover that his liver had completely regenerated itself and was now healthy.

These wonderful stories urge us not to underestimate the power of our minds, and our ability to heal our bodies and minds through visualisation.

The Spell of Self-Transformation - Your health and fitness

So what does all this mean in terms of maximising your health and fitness and achieving the relationship of your dreams? It means firstly, you understand that negative emotions and negative thinking can have a harmful influence on your body. Therefore, you know it is important to deal with these and minimise their influence. Practicing the magic and techniques in this book is helping you to do just that.

Secondly, you now know that there are actual physical benefits to be had from positive thinking and good feelings. Again, practicing techniques such as 'anchoring' in Level 3, the tools for changing your beliefs in Level 4 and the powerful psycho-remedies that follow in Level 7 will ensure that you are in the best, most resourceful, and positive emotional state you can be in.

Although stress can be a major cause of ill health, what's important is not so much that you have stressful events in your life but how you respond to them. The main health problem in modern society is that many people do not respond appropriately to the stresses in their lives. What do I mean by that? Well the stress that you experience doesn't come from outside of you but it is your mind and your body's response to the challenges you face in life.

An *appropriate* response to stress is actually beneficial.

Dr Joanne 'The Love Doctor' Coyle, Ph. D.

Thousands of years ago our ancestors would have experienced a strong sensation of fear if a ferocious wild animal jumped out at them (a stressful event!). This reaction would have been beneficial because it would have given them the energy they needed to run away. Even now, a certain amount of stress is good for you and keeps you safe. For example, it's good that you feel fear when a double-decker bus is speeding towards you, as it arouses the nervous system to propel you out of the way. Anxiety may also give you the energy boost you need when you're going for an important interview. However, remaining continually and inappropriately in a state of heightened stress strains your immune system, burns out your adrenal glands and spreads toxins throughout your body.

On any typical day you'll face any number of challenges and stressful situations. You may get stuck in a traffic jam and be late for work, you may get into an argument, your computer may crash, you may be criticised at work, you may have to pay an unexpected bill. It's important to understand that many of the things we worry about never actually happen (I'll get sacked if I disagree with my boss!) or can't be changed. Taking action to achieve your goals, meditating, exercising or practicing yoga are constructive ways of giving your mind something better to do.

People often think that they should simply avoid stressful events. That is not always easy in our modern hectic lifestyles but, as you now know, it's not the event itself but your interpretation of the event that causes emotional problems. By thinking more clearly and positively and by interpreting your experiences differently (reframing them, see Chapter 5) you can learn from your experiences and approach similar events in a calmer and more measured way.

In other words, you need to increase your capacity for handling stress to ensure that you'll perform at the peak of your abilities in all situations. How can you develop your capacity to handle stress? In his book *Stress for Success*, Dr James Loehr suggests slowly and systematically increasing exposure to stress while balancing these stressful experiences with 'quality recovery time'. The principle is the same as sports training. Exercising puts an athlete's muscles under stress. Adequate time for recovery helps the muscles to grow stronger and faster. Through this process the athlete grows stronger, fitter and more resilient. We already know that positive thinking can produce good health. All the techniques you've practiced so far in this book are magic tools to put you in the best possible state of mind for achieving your goal of a loving, supportive relationship. The mental changes you've made are already sending ripples out into your body to assist the healing process.

Practices like yoga and meditation help to calm your mind and balance your body. At the same time they help you become more aware of your body, so that you can give it what it needs. Simple yoga breathing techniques help you to deal with powerful emotions, such as fear and anger, by calming you. Yoga postures improve the functioning of all your organs and help to clear toxins from your body. Relaxation facilitates healing at the deepest level. It lowers the heart rate and the blood pressure, calms the sympathetic nervous system and relieves muscular and mental tension. Relaxation also alleviates anxiety and stress, stimulates immune function and promotes healing.

Here's what you can do to increase your resistance to stress and maximise your health and vitality and be the best you can be!

Divining the Mind

According to the Swami Sivananda,the great Indian yoga master, the fast-paced modern world has made us forget that relaxation is our natural state. Those who retain or develop the ability to relax have the key to good health, vitality and peace of mind. Relaxation is a tonic for the body and mind that unblocks and releases vast reserves of energy. You already know that your thoughts and feelings affect the functioning of your body, but the reverse is also true: the state of your body affects how you think and feel. For example, sitting slouched with your back and shoulders rounded, head down and eyes downcast is the body language of depression and will actually make you feel depressed or sad. However, if you stand erect, with your shoulders back and head up, it's impossible to feel depressed. If you don't believe me try it for yourself. Stand up right now as straight as you can, shoulders back, chest open. Look up and mentally shout, 'Yes, yes, yes, yes, yes, yes!' How do you feel (apart from a little silly)?

Because your mind affects your body and your body influences your mind, it's important to practice techniques that calm and replenish both the body and mind. Relaxation and yogic breathing are two of those techniques. If your muscles are relaxed your mind is relaxed, and if your mind is calm your body feels free and loose.

Unnecessary tension resulting from daily stresses not only causes discomfort, but drains your energy resources and can cause tiredness and ill health. Energy is being used to tell the muscles to contract and stay contracted without your being aware of it.

As you learn to relax you'll feel the tension melting away. You'll feel increasing lightness and warmth as you attain deeper and deeper states of relaxation. Be patient with yourself. It's a question of simply letting go for ten to fifteen minutes and 'not doing' rather than doing. Although you won't be aware of it, certain physiological changes will be taking place, as you relax your whole body and breathe deeply. You'll consume less oxygen and emit less carbon dioxide. Tense muscles will relax, triggering your body's natural impulse to rest, relax and recuperate, known as the parasympathetic response. Even a few minutes of deep relaxation will reduce anxiety and fatigue and restore more energy than many hours of restless sleep.

The Spell of Well Being - Energy-Giving Relaxation

1. Lie on the floor on a blanket or an exercise mat if you have one. Either stretch out your legs or bend your knees with the soles of your feet flat on the floor. Make yourself nice and comfortable.

Close your eyes.

2. Take a deep breath and let it out slowly. Breathe in and out deeply another three times and feel yourself begin to let go.

3. Now imagine a warm feeling of relaxation in your feet. Feel your feet becoming very loose and limp.

4. Let this relaxation flow into your ankles and from your ankles up your calves, over your knees and into your thighs.

5. Imagine your legs being completely relaxed. Allow the feeling of relaxation to spread from your thighs into your hips and from your hips into all the muscles and organs of your pelvis and deeper into your abdomen.

6. Continue to breathe deeply and with each exhalation let your body become more relaxed.

7. Imagine the feeling of relaxation flowing up all the muscles of your back, into your shoulders and down into your chest, so that all the muscles of your chest are relaxed.

8. Allow the feeling to flow down your arms to your elbows, from your elbows to your wrists and from your wrists into your hands, going out to the ends of your fingertips.

9. Feel the relaxation flow up all the muscles of your neck and into your head. Let the warm feeling flow down into your brow and your eyes and feel all the muscles of your face relax.

10. Take three more deep breaths and send the exhalation to any part of the body that is not yet relaxed. Feel your body soften and let go.

Stay with this feeling as long as you wish. If at some point you find that your attention has wandered and you want to rest completely, that's perfectly okay. Enjoy your time to relax. Relax for five to fifteen minutes and you'll arise refreshed and energised.

Calming Yogic Breathing

1. Sit comfortably with your spine erect. Settle down and close your eyes. Bring your awareness to your breathing.

2. Simply notice how you're breathing. Are you breathing

quickly or slowly? Is your breathing deep or shallow? Simply observe your breathing for two to three minutes without changing it.

3. As you breathe in count one and as you breathe out count two, so that you're lengthening the exhalation. Continue breathing in for one count and out for two for five rounds of breathing.

4. Breathe in for a count of two and out for a count of four. Do this five times.

5. Breathe in for three counts and out for six. Again, do this five times.

6. Breathe in for four counts and out for eight, five times.

7. Breathe in for three and out for six, five times.

8. Breathe in for two and out for four, five times.

9. Breathe in for one and out for two, five times.

10. Allow your breathing to return to normal and notice how you feel.

The Spell of Essential Self-Love

Any form of healing starts with love. Healing means to make whole, and love always seeks to make whole. A wealth of scientific evidence demonstrates that care and compassion can protect living beings from many diseases.

Researchers at Ohio University of Medicine examined the effects of a high-fat, high-cholesterol diet on rabbits. The scientists monitored the rabbits, looking for evidence of arteriosclerosis. The symptoms of arteriosclerosis include the clogging, narrowing and hardening of the large arteries and blood vessels that can lead to stroke, heart attack, eye problems and kidney problems. The scientists had expected the level of arteriosclerosis to be high in all the rabbits, but one group had 60 percent less atherosclerosis than any other group. Eventually the researchers discovered that a technician had taken these rabbits out of their cages and stroked them every day. The amazing findings were confirmed by a repeat experiment. This act of care and compassion again reduced atherosclerosis by 60 percent. It had significantly changed the biology of the rabbits, protecting them from the harmful effects of their high-fat, high-cholesterol diet!

If care and compassion and touch can do this for rabbits, then think what it can do for human beings. Being caressed lowers blood pressure and releases natural opiates in the human brain. In fact, the absence of touching can cause many animals, including humans, to die early. Love and touch helps children to grow and develop. Scientific studies have found that children who grow up in a loving and nurturing environment develop larger, denser, prefrontal lobes, than children raised in emotionally deprived homes. Dense prefrontal lobes contain a multitude of communication connections to different parts of the brain which enable children to communicate freely and clearly. Fear, anxiety and a sense of isolation resulting from continued neglect can suppress specific genes, so that a child's growth is slowed down or even stopped.

Being lovingly touched satisfies a basic human need: it can comfort us, support us, protect and encourage us. It can also arouse and relax us. We have an eternal desire for touch and it is one of our strongest needs. It is the reason we continue to search for someone special to satisfy this requirement.

In general, love encourages mental and physical health. You'll have far greater success in healing yourself and promoting your health if you love and care for yourself. Love is about loving people just the way they are. Loving yourself means the same thing, loving yourself just the way *you* are. The following techniques are powerful spells for making you feel appreciated, cared for and loved.

Seeing Yourself with Love

1.   Close your eyes and go back to a time when you felt loved or deeply appreciated. See what you saw, hear what you heard and feel those feelings of love rise up within you. Double the feeling.

Now treble it.

2. When the feelings are at their strongest, press the first knuckle of your left hand with your right index finger.

3. Think of a person who loves you or really appreciates you. Recall how that person looks and see him or her standing in front of you now.

4. Float out of your own body and into the body of the person who appreciates you. See through that person's eyes, hear through that person's ears and feel the love and appreciation he or she feels for you. See the amazing qualities that you possibly hadn't recognised in yourself until now.

5. Now float back into your own body and take a few minutes to enjoy, knowing that you're loved and appreciated just the way you are.

The next spell, called 'The Good Samaritan', is another great tool for making you feel appreciated and valued. You're going to remember times when you've shown another person kindness or done them a favour no matter how small. One reason this technique works so well is that everyone has done something at some time to help someone else. Even if you can't think of anything at the moment, you can always go out and do something for someone else then come back and do the exercise! It's that easy. Appreciation from others helps you see qualities in yourself that you might not see otherwise.

The Good Samaritan

1. Close your eyes and remember a time when you helped someone out and felt appreciated. Run through the experience in vivid detail. Recall the person's appreciation. See how the person looks; hear what he or she says.

2. Step out of your body and into the body of the person who appreciates you. See what that person saw, hear what he or she heard and feel that person's feelings towards you.

3. Step back into your own body and feel your own feelings of gratitude, knowing you're deeply appreciated.

4. Resolve to perform more small acts of kindness as you go about your daily life.

When you give, whether it is your time, your money or a gift, you are unconsciously acknowledging that 'you have'. You must 'have' or you would not be able to give. By focusing on 'I have' you are attracting even more things 'to have'. So be generous in giving. Give others the material things you are able to give, and also give authentically of yourself. Listen to others, give them your time, your patience, your compassion and, where it is needed, your forgiveness. They will value you and appreciate you for this. Notice how good you feel when you give. When you give those things you also attract them to you.

Be grateful for all the good things in your life. Every morning when I get up, I spend fifteen minutes focussing on everything I am grateful for. Even if your life is not yet great, there are always small things you can appreciate. It might be a lovely sunny day, a flower, a neighbour saying 'hello', chatting with a stranger. I find that once I think of one thing, others start to pop into my head and I realise there are many things in my life I am grateful for. I can't think of a better way to start the day. Being grateful is one of the most powerful ways to attract love into your life. Being grateful even for the smallest things will attract more things you can be grateful for.

Divining the Spirit

Another great way to relax and cope with stress is meditation, which helps to still your mind and balance your emotions. Meditation can also help you solve problems by giving you insights. It can take you to higher states of awareness, peace and clarity. Meditation means to 'become familiar with'. It is a way of discovering your inner self. In the busy world around you, where your senses are continually drawn outward, meditation gives you a wonderful opportunity to turn inward on a journey of self-discovery.

There are many techniques of meditation, some of which are

described in this Level. Try them out and find the ones that you like best. Keeping a journal of your personal discoveries and experiences will enhance your progress in meditation.

Preparation

Find the time that best fits your routine and practice meditation for five to ten minutes each day. Have a special place for your meditation. As you practice in this place you'll find it becomes calmer and more peaceful, so that even entering your special place makes you feel relaxed and focused. You can sit comfortably in a chair or on the floor with your legs crossed, or you can lie down flat or with your knees bent. The most important thing is that you're comfortable because you'll be in that position anywhere from five to fifteen minutes. Make sure your spine and neck are straight and your shoulders are relaxed.

The Spell of Peace - Meditation for Peace and Harmony

1. Turn your attention inwards. Spend a few moments listening to your body and feeling how you feel.
2. Bring your attention to the tip of your nose and notice the breath as it goes in and out of your body. Gently breathe in and out through your nose. Focusing on the tip of your nose, take another few minutes to follow the flow of your breath in and out of your body.
3. Begin to breathe more deeply. Take long, slow inhalations, filling up your lungs completely, and then let the air out slowly. Stay with the breath several minutes more. Then allow your breathing to return to its natural rhythm.
4. Mentally scan your body and notice any areas that aren't yet relaxed. Breathe in deeply and as you breathe out allow your breath to flow into these areas, relaxing them as it goes.
5. Move your attention slowly through your body from your head down to your toes. Be with each part for a moment, and then let that part relax. Accept each part, however it feels.

6. When your whole body is relaxed, become aware of your feelings. Be with each feeling for a moment, and then let it go. You're a passive observer of your feelings.
7. Imagine a clear, clean stream of water washing your feelings away. Let this pure, cleansing water flow through you, washing each feeling away until you feel peace and clarity within.
8. Notice any thoughts that pass through your mind and let them go. Imagine a fresh breeze blowing through your mind, leaving it empty and clear.
9. Finally, allow yourself to rest in stillness. Be aware that each time you practice this meditation you'll receive greater benefits.

The following meditation helps you to enhance your five senses and to fully experience what's going on around you and within you. This technique allows you to experience the fullness of being in the present moment.

The Spell for Heightened Awareness - Five Senses Meditation

1. Close your eyes and begin by breathing deeply. Take long slow inhalations, filling up your lungs completely, and then let the air out slowly. Stay with your breath several minutes more, then allow your breathing to return to its natural rhythm.
2. Bring your awareness to your sense of smell. Be aware of what you can smell from moment to moment for two or three minutes. If your mind wanders, gently bring it back to this focus.
3. Focus on your sense of taste. What do you taste on your tongue? Elsewhere in your mouth? Stay with your sense of taste for two to three minutes.
4. Bring your attention to your vision. Open your eyes and see what you can see. Be attentive for two or three minutes. Notice everything you can see: the colours, the shapes, and the light.
5. Close your eyes again and be aware of your sense of touch. Feel the contact of your body with the chair or floor. Feel the clothes against your skin. Feel the air on your bare skin. Open yourself to your sense of touch for two or three minutes.
6. Tune in to your sense of hearing. Listen to all the sounds

from far away. Hear the sounds in your immediate space. Tune in to the sounds of your body; listen carefully for two or three minutes.

7. Now turn inwards and rest in stillness. Allow yourself simply to be.

8. After several minutes take some long, slow, deep breaths and open your eyes. Resolve to be aware of your senses and use them much more as you go about your daily business.

The Spell for Creativity - Visualisation Meditation

The next meditative exercise helps you to develop your imagination and creativity.

1. Sit or lie comfortably and take some long, slow, deep breaths.
2. Mentally scan your body and allow each part to relax. Breathe into any areas of the body that aren't yet relaxed.
3. Once you feel relaxed, imagine you're standing on a beach.
4. See the white sand around you and the clear blue sky above you. Notice the sunlight glinting off the water. Observe the branches of the trees swaying in the gentle breeze.
5. Hear the waves lapping onto the shore. Hear the swish of the trees and the calls of the seabirds flying overhead.
6. Feel the warm sand between your toes and the sun warming your head and shoulders. Feel the breeze blowing through your hair.
7. Smell and taste the salty air.
8. Be aware of the atmosphere; go for a walk or a swim. Feel what it's like to be actually there.
9. Return to the present by becoming aware of your body. Take some long, slow, deep breaths to waken your body. Feel the contact of the floor or chair supporting your body and hear the sounds around you. When you're ready open your eyes.

Divining the Body - Good Exercise and Good Diet

Having read this far you will already understand that the body and mind are one, and that the body influences the mind and the mind affects the body. Everyday challenges can produce tension in your body. Your body can generate a stress response where your muscles contract and adrenaline pumps through your body. Relaxation is one way to release this tension. Another is exercise. When you find ways of releasing the tension produced by the stress response, your body will feel calmer, stronger and healthier. Your mind will be calmer too, helping you think more clearly, relax more easily and sleep more soundly.

I'm not telling you to go out and run a marathon or rush down to the nearest gym, but finding some form of exercise that you enjoy is vital. If you exercise just for the sake of exercise you're more likely to let other things get in the way, and soon you'll be beating yourself up for not sticking to your regime.

First, find something you enjoy doing. It could be walking, it could be salsa dancing, or it could be swimming, sailing, and yoga, whatever! Get out of the house. Go to classes and meet people. Ask around about the best classes to go to. I love yoga and would recommend anyone to try it. It's suitable for everyone and can be adapted for every level, from the absolute beginner to the practiced yogi. I also love to walk and cycle. I'm fortunate that I can cycle to work. Sticking to my exercise regime is easy because I love the things I do. I can't wait to get out on my bike or out walking in the fresh air, and I love the way I feel after a relaxing yoga session. If you find what you love, exercising becomes easy!

Try to use your car less often. Make little changes in your routine so that you do more walking. Either don't take the car to work, or park some distance away from your destination, so that you can walk there and back. Take every opportunity you can to walk. Walk up and down stairs rather than taking the elevator. Get out of the office or the house and walk around the block or further. Get moving as much as you can during your day. Notice the difference it makes.

Here's a great way to motivate yourself. It's the same process we did in Level 2 to discover what motivates you in relationships, when you discovered your relationship values. It's a Spell to get motivated to do exercise! Discover your health and fitness values

1. Take a sheet of paper and ask yourself, 'What's important to me about my health or being healthy?' Quickly write down whatever comes to mind. Ask yourself, 'What else is important to me about being healthy? What else, what else..?' and so on. Write down all the words and phrases you come up with until you feel you've exhausted the subject.
2. Rest for a few moments, then ask yourself again, 'What's important to me about my health?' You'll find that more words pop into your head. Write those down too.
3. Look at all the values you've written and ask yourself, 'If I could have only one value that's most important for my health and fitness, what would it be? What's most important to me?' Write your answer on a separate piece of paper.
4. Ask yourself, 'If I could have only one more value out of all of these, what would it be?' Note that one underneath your response to question 3. 'If I could have one more, which one would it be?' Repeat this step until you've elicited five values.

Good, you've now discovered your values for your health and well-being. Read them back to yourself and ask, 'If my level of health and fitness enabled me to satisfy all these values would I be happy?' These values are what drives and motivates you in terms of health. Choose a large and bold font and print out these values on a sheet of paper. Place them in a prominent location where you'll see them regularly such as on your fridge door. Every time you go out to exercise look at this sheet of paper.

Now, go back to Level 2 and review the section called 'The Keys to Achieving Your Goals'. Set a goal for your health and fitness and go for it! Make sure the goal you've set for yourself is in alignment with your values, that is, it helps satisfy one or more of your health values. If your health values and goals are aligned, you'll find that achieving your goals are easy. Go for it!

Spell for Eating Like a Naturally Thin Person

As far as diet is concerned, you'll be surprised to hear me say that in countries like the United Kingdom people are probably eating less than they did fifty years ago, with the exception of the enormous portions we're faced with when we eat out. But generally we're eating less than our grandparents and great-grandparents did. Yet people in the United Kingdom and other Western countries are getting bigger and heavier. Obesity is becoming a major public health concern because of the diseases associated with it, such as type two diabetes, heart disease and stroke. The problem isn't so much that we're eating more, it's just that we're exercising less and burning up fewer calories than ever before.

The equation for the normal weight for your size, sex and shape is simple: Your input (food) must be appropriate for your output (physical activity). If you want to be trim or within the normal range, your eating must reflect the energy you need for your life-style. If you have an active life with lots of strenuous activities you need a lot of fuel (food) to run on. If your life is less active, say you drive to work, sit in front of a computer screen all day and drive home - you'll need far fewer calories.

The good news is that you can choose. You can change either side of the food/exercise equation to bring you closer to the kind of body you want. If you're overweight, you can either increase your exercise levels to bring you into line with what you're eating, or you can reduce your food intake to bring it into line with your activity level. Or you can change both your diet and your exercise regime.

A good way of finding out what your body needs is simply to listen to your body and be aware of how you're feeling. Notice when you're genuinely feeling hungry. We all get into bad habits of eating when we are not hungry. We end up eating at certain times of the day, eating because we are bored, eating because other people are eating. What we now have to do is listen to our body and eat when we are hungry. So you must learn to notice the signs of genuine hunger. Every time you sit down to eat, ask yourself, 'Am I really hungry?' You'll need to recognise the difference between real (actual physical) hunger and emotional hunger. Physical hunger is gradual; you may become aware of gentle stirrings in your stomach or a deep rumbling. These are gentle physical hints that you really are hungry.

Emotional hunger is a sudden and urgent feeling, while physical hunger is a gradual, growing feeling. Think back to a time when you've had a sudden desperate craving for food. It is likely you were upset, you had an argument with someone or you were feeling bad about yourself. People often try to smother unpleasant feelings with food, so that they don't have to look at them or deal with them. Emotional hunger/upset cannot be satisfied with food.

If you are eating and never feel satisfied that's because you don't need the food. What you need to do is change your feelings. Get up and move, go out for a walk or deal with the emotions. If it takes going to a therapist or counsellor to resolve the feelings, then do so. Once you resolve the root cause of emotional hunger, you will no longer use food to deal with emotional problems.

Notice the difference between a physical state like hunger and an emotional state, such as boredom or feeling low. You should eat what you want, not what you think you should. This is sound advice and will help you begin to follow your natural instincts about what you want. If you listen to your body over a period of time it will let you know what it wants and needs. If your body tells you that you need a slice of cheesecake, then have it! But remember it is your body that you are listening to, not your mind! It is about being sensitive to your body and noticing how you feel. If you do this, remarkably you will end up with a balanced diet without realising it. You will also notice your tastes changing as you go on.

Don't eat when you're in a hurry or while you're standing or walking. Take your time and sit down to eat. Chew each mouthful thoroughly Keep you full attention on your food when you are eating. You can eat whatever you want whenever but you must fully appreciate and savour every single mouthful. Give your food your full attention. Really enjoy it, savour the taste, the texture and chew each mouthful. For the next two to three weeks slow your eating speed down to about a quarter of what it used to be and chew each mouthful thoroughly.

Listen to your body so that you recognise when you're full. The human body is naturally designed to eat when we're hungry and stop when we're satisfied, but many of us have got into the habit of overruling our body and eating until we're bursting or until we clean our plate. To lose weight in an easy way and keep it off you must work with your body and not against it. We need to re-sensitise ourselves to our 'inner thermostat'. That is, we need to notice (and feel) when we are full, stop eating and then we get on with our day. The next time you are eating, take your awareness to the area just below your ribcage and above your tummy (solar plexus). Notice if you feel full. If you do, you can stop eating.

Go out and buy a journal and keep track of what you're eating, when and where you're eating and how much you're spending on food. By simply keeping a record of your behaviour you'll begin to notice unhelpful patterns that you'll want to break. Be guided by what your body needs. Be sensitive to what's going on in your body. Eat plenty of fresh fruit and vegetables. Observe how you feel forty-five to sixty minutes after eating. Be aware of whether you feel energised and clear headed or lethargic and unmotivated. Learn which high-energy foods are healthy for you. By completing your diary and practicing this technique for a week you can design a diet that's perfect for your unique body.

If you follow this simple advice you will behave differently around food. You'll feel relaxed and good about what you eat, and you'll feel in control of your eating. In a short while you will achieve and maintain a weight and body shape that you are happy with and is perfect for you.

Finally, if there are foodstuffs which you would really like to cut from your diet, like chocolate, sweets and crisps, or sugary fizzy drinks, then here's a great spell.

The Yuck Spell!

Let's call the food or drink you wish to stop consuming X. Please read through the instructions fully and make sure you understand all the steps before using this technique.

1. Think of a smell that you find totally disgusting. You must either clearly remember it or vividly imagine it for this spell to work really well. For example, can you imagine how your toilet would smell if it hadn't been flushed for a week? Or for those of you who have been to festivals imagine the smell of a 'portaloo' after a week! Just imagine that rotten eggy and urine smell. Or any other smell that makes you feel totally disgusted.
2. Now imagine or remember that awful smell – what you notice as you breathe it in and how disgusted you feel. As the feelings well up within you, squeeze together the thumb and middle finger of your **left hand**. Repeat this process as many times as you need to feel utterly revolted. Keep going until you are actually gagging.
3. Next remember a taste you find utterly disgusting - it can be food or drink. You need something that makes you feel really quite sick. How disgusting would it be to drink someone else's sick in a basin, or perhaps the contents of a spittoon? What if it was filled with plenty of big green juicy lumps of phlegm? Squeeze thumb and middle finger of your **left hand** and imagine swallowing that disgusting substance. Keep doing it again and again until you feel you're going to puke.
4. Now as you squeeze your left thumb and finger together, remembering how disgusting that smell and tasted, imagine eating/drinking a little bit of X, then a bit more and more, gradually increasing the amount of X. Imagine that each time you eat/drink X, a little bit more of that disgusting smell and taste is getting mixed together with the smell and taste of X.
5. Keep repeating this process until you can no longer find anything but repulsion in the idea of eating/drinking X.

A Positive Enchantment - A Healthy Attitude

There is much truth in the old adage 'a sound mind in a sound body'. In this Level you learned a number of ways to promote your health and well-being. Rest assured that all the techniques you've practiced so far in this book are benefiting you by helping you to think more positively about your relationships and your life. Try out all the energy-giving and health-giving techniques in this Level and find the ones you really like. Allow them to become part of your daily routine. Notice how much more relaxed and calm you feel and how much more confident and energised you are.

Most psychologists' definition of a successful life is one where there is balance and where the person is able to love and accept themselves with all their fallibilities as well as their strengths. It is vital for the individual to be true to themselves and, through being themselves, to create relationships and opportunities that bring happiness and joy to those around them. You may think this sounds a little fanciful, but the truth is that by learning to love and accept ourselves, we are also learning to love and accept others. We now know that it is really not possible to have the one without the other.

Feeling attractive, energised and confident will attract others to you. You will exude an inner radiance and sense of well being that will change how others relate to you. You will also have the calm assurance that you can achieve your goal of attaining the relationship of your dreams because you truly deserve it.

Your Practical Magic for Level 6

1. Practice the energy-giving relaxation technique and the calming yoga breathing technique.
2. Elicit your values for your health and fitness (review the procedure in Level 2). Set a goal for your health and fitness.
3. Start doing a physical activity that you enjoy.
4. Keep a journal of your eating habits for two weeks.
5. Meditate for five to fifteen minutes at the same time each day for one week.

You have now made profound life changes. Notice the way in which everything around you is now changing for the better. On completion of the above tasks, please proceed to Level 7.

Level 7

Put the Past to Rest – Healing and Beyond

It's easy enough to understand that when you love and value yourself you will attract love and respect, and when you criticise yourself you will attract disrespect and lack of acceptance. So all we need to do is love and accept ourselves to become irresistible to the opposite sex. It sounds so easy. Yet loving and accepting ourselves is probably the most difficult thing we can ever learn to do.

In order to love ourselves we must first accept and forgive ourselves and in the process accept and forgive others. The bedrock of self- love is self-healing. You may have endured the heartbreak of splitting up with partners or lovers, or you may have noticed some painful recurring patterns in your relationships. Maybe you haven't been involved in a relationship for some time, or maybe you yearn for a loving, stable relationship but can't seem to find one. If any of these statements apply to you, something within you needs to be healed and is holding you back from getting the type of relationship you desire.

Looking into the Magic Dish - Why Is My Love Life the Way It Is?

Have you thought about why your relationships have been unsatisfying or unsuccessful? About why you chose a particular person and not someone else or why that person chose you? Have you asked yourself whether there's a definite pattern to your relationships or why you haven't had a relationship for a while? By now you have had an inkling that it hasn't just been coincidence or bad luck.

Your behaviour is determined by many factors, many of which you're unaware of. But psychologists generally agree that the *imprinting* you received from your family as a small child has more influence on your adult relationships and choice of partners than anything else.

It is usually within our families that we experience our first significant relationships. By observing how people treat you and relate to each other, you begin to weave together a story of what relationships are all about. As a child, you receive a variety of unconscious messages from those around you, which you later take with you into adult life.

Later in adulthood, intimate relationships, more than any other, can propel us right back to childhood and old feelings of hurt, sadness and anger. When we feel our partner is not meeting our emotional needs, it can press all the old buttons. Our relationships give us a chance to exorcise the old emotional ghosts and scars from our childhood. This is because when we fall in love, we are often unconsciously attracted to partners who posses the characteristics and qualities of our parents. We have a second chance to work them through, know ourselves better and forgive our parents if we need to.

The reason childhood experiences are so powerful is that when you're a baby your home and family are your whole world. You have no knowledge of anything outside those limits. Because you have no basis of comparison, what you see, hear and feel around you is simply how things are. Your parents' relationship shows how men and women treat each other, and relations between you and your family show how people relate to each other. Your first impressions of these relationships are imprinted in your unconscious mind before you can think to question them.

You learned a whole range of feelings, beliefs and behaviours from your family. For example, are you the type who feels insecure? Do you feel easily rejected? Do you find it hard to make a commitment? Do you often feel jealous of those the same sex as you? Many such issues can be traced back to childhood.

If you came from a family in which you felt loved and secure, you'll probably find it easy to trust people as an adult. However, if you felt rejected, unloved, or lost someone close to you, you may find it harder to believe that others will love you, stay with you and treat you well.

It is very important to be able to trust adult relationships. If things have happened in your past that have undermined your ability to trust, you may find you need the understanding and support of a partner to rebuild your faith in others.

From these childhood observations you formed your beliefs about how men should treat women and how women should treat men. You learned how to behave in public and private and how to respond to your needs and desires and to those of others. How family members treated you helps determine your estimate of your own self-worth, what you expect from life, what you think you deserve and how or whether your needs should be met. Your beliefs about love and how to show it also come from your family. Even though you've grown up, left your original family and developed new friendships and lifestyles, that family still provides the template for most of your intimate relationships.

If you find it is easy to show your emotions, you were probably raised in an environment where you and other family members were encouraged to be open about how you felt. Most likely you saw other people venting anger or crying, and saw them make up, too. You learned that disagreement and conflict is not the end of the world and that communicating how you are feeling can make life better.

Relationships are healthy when individuals can express themselves honestly and appropriately. It can be just as unhealthy to be brought up in a family where disputes are ignored as it is to be brought up in an angry pressure cooker.

A range of psychological theories attempts to explain how the experiences and relationships you're exposed to in childhood come to be replicated when you're grown up. For example, one influential theory suggests that we try to get from our partners what we didn't get from our parents. For example, if your parents praised you a lot and encouraged all your efforts, most likely you'll grow up to be confident in your abilities. You'll also be happy to try to develop new skills or try new ventures. If another child's parents seldom praised her, ignored and discouraged her, most likely she feels insecure about her capabilities and unconfident about her decisions. Since she feels uncertain about her own judgments she may look to others for reassurance. As an adult she may turn to partners for the comfort and encouragement she didn't receive from her parents.

The strongest influence, therefore, from your family is the imprint of your parents' relationship. Their behaviour towards each other acts as a template for how you set about creating your own relationships.

Anne Teachworth, a gestalt therapist practicing couple counselling for more than twenty years, discovered that as adults we have an unconscious drive to replicate our parents' relationship because at an unconscious level that's what we expect a relationship to be. Even if we wouldn't consciously desire that type of relationship, we unconsciously look for partners who will help us replicate those patterns.

According to Teachworth, you take on the role of one parent or the other, not necessarily the parent of the same sex, in your own relationships. Typically, the role you choose is that of the parent you prefer. Your unconscious mind looks out for someone who can play the role of the other parent. If your parents had troubles and conflicts you may be vulnerable to similar problems. When adults grow up finding it difficult to cope with sharing or competition, often the root of the problem is a family where authority and control were badly managed.

If as a child you learned that sharing was fun and there was plenty to go around, as an adult you'll enjoy sharing. If as a child you were taught things were scarce, then as an adult you may be more inclined to keep things to yourself. If your parents helped you to understand that certain rules were in your best interests, you are likely see rules as necessary and have few problems with authority.

When we feel we have control over our lives, our sense of

self-confidence grows. If a child is given responsibility from an early age they are more likely to grow up feeling self-confident about their decisions and they can make mistakes and learn from their mistakes.

During the highly impressionable imprint phase when your family and home were your whole world you probably made many unconscious decisions about relationships, other people and yourself. Some of these decisions may have helped to make you a confident adult. Others may have had a less than happy influence on your life and relationships.

So psychologists are agreed that we learn what being a couple is about from watching our parents.

If you were brought up in a single-parent family, you will also have expectations from observing the relationships your parent was in, or you will have ideas about what being alone is like.

Whatever your background, you'll have absorbed important lessons about:

- How much affection couples can show each one another and when and where they can do this
- What things couples disagree about and how they resolve disagreements
- How much time they should spend together and what they do together
- Who's decision is final
- Who earns the money, who controls it and who spends it
- Activities that women are better at than men and vice versa
- Who has responsibility for domestic chores
- How sex is viewed
- The way men and women express anger or sadness
- How to celebrate family events and special occasions
- Whether it's better to be in a couple than to be single

Fortunately, because of advances in the psycho-technologies

of Neuro-Linguistic Programming (NLP), and the discovery of magical psychological tools contained in traditional Huna, you're now in a position to change the unconscious patterns that you bring to relationships. These two imaginative approaches offer ways to disconnect problem patterns, so that they can no longer adversely affect your relationships.

The Healing Spell - The Emotional Healing Process

The techniques I'm about to share with you are the most powerful and effective ways I know to get at the root cause of any problems you've been experiencing in relationships and dissolve any troubling emotions associated with them. Before I take you through these processes, I'd like to say to anyone who's going through a painful break up that we have a natural, in-built method for dealing with loss, called the grieving process. If you're mourning the loss of a relationship or partner give yourself time, care for yourself and look towards healing yourself through the techniques described later in this Level.

You don't have to pretend you are strong, stoic or invulnerable. Your emotions and your hopes for the future are as important and valuable, as everyone else's. If the future you hoped for is no longer tenable, you have suffered a real loss, it is significant and you have a right to grieve. If you have lost a dream you will feel hurt. You are also worth it and deserve to get over this pain. Don't be embarrassed to admit you feel hurt. Those who deny or suppress their sadness do not grieve for it and therefore do not move on.

The emotional healing process has five stages. This grieving process will allow you to let go of your attachment to that particular person. The stages you're going through are natural. Just allow them to pass, noticing your feelings and how they've changed on the way. Recognise where you are and be ready to move on when the time is right for you.

Stage 1: Denial

Initially, you may be shocked by the break up and find it difficult to comprehend. You may deny that the break up happened and want to get back with your former partner. Instead of feeling down you may be waiting for your ex-partner to come back and for everything to be okay. Maybe you feel numb. If so you're in denial. Let yourself feel the shock and numbness. Sit with it for a little while. Talk your feelings through with a close friend or counsellor. Recognise that you're in denial and let it pass.

Stage 2: Fear
In this phase, you may feel like you've reached the end of your dreams. You may wonder whether you'll ever feel better, whether you'll be able to trust anyone again. You may blow everything out of proportion as you project all your fears and doubts into the future. If you feel afraid about the future it's important to recognise that your fears are groundless, if you're prepared to change the beliefs and behaviour that determine your future. Focus on 'now' at this stage. Take one day at a time.

Stage 3: Anger
Anger is a natural emotion. It's only natural that you're angry with your partner for leaving or for not being the person that you wanted him or her to be. You may also be angry with yourself for not picking up that things were going wrong sooner. You may feel angry at the whole world at this moment. NLP techniques can help you to reduce the power of inappropriate anger by disconnecting it from all your memories. You may still feel anger, but you'll feel an appropriate level of anger connected specifically to this experience, rather than a welling of anger from distant experiences deep in your unconscious mind. You can express appropriate anger in a suitable way at a suitable time and place, such as punching a punch bag or getting out for a run or cycle or talking to a friend.

Stage 4: Depression

You may feel depressed and unhappy. You may feel that you'll never be happy again. Like every other stage, this one will pass. You need to take care of yourself here. You must do whatever you can to nurture and comfort yourself. You must pay particular attention to your physical health, eating as healthily as possible and taking light but vigorous exercise, preferably outdoors where you can take in fresh air. Yoga is particularly good for relaxing the body and calming the mind.

Again, NLP techniques can help you to reduce the power of sadness through disconnecting inappropriate sadness and hurt from all your memories. This isn't to say that you'll feel completely happy. Rather, you'll feel an appropriate level of sadness and loss related solely to this time and experience, instead of sadness permeating the unconscious mind from earlier experiences. NLP techniques and the psychology of Huna make the grieving process much easier, cleaner and quicker through allowing you to grieve for that particular relationship rather than unconsciously grieving for every loss you've ever suffered.

Stage 5: Acceptance
You've been on an emotional roller coaster and it's time to get off. Your break up is in the past. It's behind you. You've learned more about yourself and what you want in life. You've let go of the relationship and you're ready to move on to something new and different. You recognise how much you've learned and changed as you went through the emotional healing process. Your emotions are healed, and you'll be much stronger and more comfortable in dealing with any future challenges.

Many people often do not recognise their own part in the breakdown of a relationship and are quick to blame their partners. They may simply move on to a new relationship where they typically repeat the same mistakes because they have not learned or gained any insight to do things differently. They may actually feel that staying single is the safest thing to do. It is a great way of avoiding the hurt and conflict that an intimate relationship can bring through its very closeness and intimacy. But you have to think, is it what you really want?

Whether you're currently going through the process of emotional healing or you've noticed recurring self-destructive patterns in your relationships, the following psychological spells will help you. They are powerful ways of getting rid of any harmful beliefs and unwanted emotions that may be holding you back from achieving the relationship of your dreams. The first potion will help you to dissolve anger, sadness, fear and guilt and to dispel any self-defeating beliefs and decisions you've unconsciously made about relationships. The second spell will help you to resolve any inner conflicts you may have about yourself or relationships. The final piece of magic will help you to understand more about yourself and to see others and your relationships more clearly. Read all the instructions carefully before trying the spells. Take your time and work through these exercises fully. You'll be amazed at the results!

The Spell for Dissolving negative beliefs and unwanted emotions

Developed after years of research, this first spell is widely acknowledged as one of the most powerful and effective methods for creating quick and lasting change in people's lives.

Your past determines who you are and how you act. As I mentioned earlier, your memories are stored in your unconscious mind in a particular sequence and around a particular theme, for example, happy memories, unhappy memories, guilty memories and so on. As adults our behaviour and the feelings we have in the present is often a reaction to a gestalt, a collection of memories from our past. In other words, how we act and how we feel is unconsciously guided by decisions and feelings we've made or had in the past.

I am about to share with you an amazing technique that will enable you to change the meaning you give to your memories so that they no longer have the power to hold you back or generate unhappiness or hurt in your life.

Here's how it works. Firstly, you answer the 'Lynch pin' questionnaire, to discover the root cause of your problem. Then you release the problem pattern and negative emotions through the 'The Magic Wand – Problem Banisher'.

Step 1 - The Lynch Pin Questionnaire
Sit comfortably and relax. Now answer the following questionnaire. Be absolutely honest with yourself. Trust yourself. Find the 'lynch pin' of your problems. You will know when you have found the lynch pin of what is holding you back from getting the relationship you really want, when something incredibly simple just pops into your mind such as 'I'm not good enough', 'I can't be loved', 'I'm bad'. It will be a revelation for you and you will know that you have found what you are looking for. It will be accompanied by a feeling that you have found the real problem that has eluded you for so long. It is very important you take your time with this process, so set aside at least one hour.

1. If you could have anything as a result of practicing all the techniques in this book, what would you want?
2. What do you currently have in your life that you no longer want?
3. What do you not have in your life that you now want?
4. Write down any events that were significant to you in your life (positive and negative)
5. What patterns have you noticed recurring in your life so far?
6. Why are you reading this book? (Give as many reasons as you can.) Keep asking yourself 'Why else?', 'Why else?'
7. If this problem were to disappear right now for good, how would you know it had gone?
8. How do you know you have this problem?
9. How long have you had this problem?
10. Was there ever a time when you didn't have this problem?
11. What happened the first time you had this?
12. What happened since?

13. What emotions do you associate with this problem?
14. What do you believe about your problem?
15. Describe your childhood in relation to this problem.
16. Describe your family, father, mother, brothers and sisters in relation to this problem.
17. Ask your unconscious mind when did you decide to create this problem and for what purpose?
18. Ask your unconscious mind if there is anything your unconscious mind wants you to pay attention to such that, if you were to pay attention to it, it would cause the problem to disappear.
19. What is it that you are not doing because you have this problem?
20. Ask your unconscious mind if it is totally willing for you to have an undeniable experience of this problem disappearing today?

Now we have got to the root cause of your problem, 'the lynch pin' problem. When you resolve this, your problem will disappear and the negative emotions associated with it. Here's how you can do this...proceed to step 2.

Step 2 The Magic Wand – Problem Banisher
1. Okay, well done. Now just sit and relax. Take a deep breathe in through your nose, fill up your lungs completely, hold it, then breathe out through your nose slowly. Repeat another three times.
2. Now ask your unconscious mind what is the root cause of this problem, the first event that when disconnected, will cause the problem to disappear? How old were you when you decided to have this problem? Just allow whatever memory or picture to pop into your mind. It doesn't matter how irrelevant or silly it may at first seem. The first thing that pops into your head is usually right.
3. Now go back to that time, the first event in which the problem appeared. Make sure you really are at the first event. If you are not sure, then ask your unconscious mind. 'Is this the first event? Or is there an earlier one than this? Go back to the FIRST one.'

4. Good. Now imagine you are sitting in a cinema and you are going to watch yourself in the event up on the screen.

5. Okay, now run the movie of you in the event in black and white on the screen. Just sit in the cinema and watch yourself.

6. At the end of the movie, freeze frame it then have it white out completely.

7. Now step inside the movie where it ended. This time you are in the movie. Be sure you are looking out through your own eyes this time. Now run the movie backwards in colour until you reach the very beginning.

8. Repeat steps 3-6 until you can't get that old feeling back at all or until the memory and decision is not longer accessible to you…no matter how hard you try!

9. Take a deep breathe in through your nose, fill up your lungs completely, hold it, then breathe out through your nose slowly. Repeat another three times.

10. Bring your awareness to the tip of your nose and simply notice your breath as it goes in and out of your body. Gently focus on your breath in this way for the next five minutes. Then simply notice how you feel.

Well done. You can now use this process to bust any problem patterns that you become aware of regarding your relationships and any other area of your life. It is also excellent for releasing fear and phobias.

Don't worry if following these steps feels a little strange at first. You can use 'The Magic Wand – Problem Banisher' to get rid of troubling emotions too. Simply focus on the negative feeling, e.g. sadness, and work through all the instructions in 'The Magic Wand' technique. You'll notice that moving towards your goal of a loving relationship is becoming easier and easier. The more you use this technique, the more your unconscious mind will know what it's being asked to do and the easier it will become.

The Spell for Becoming Whole

Sometimes we experience problems in achieving the loving relationship we've always wanted because unconscious parts of ourselves want different, incompatible things. You may be vaguely aware of conflicting ideas about what you want in a relationship. Part of you may want security and another part may want the opposite, the stress of lack of security. You may even discover that, 'A part of me says, it's not okay to have a loving relationship' or 'A part of me says I don't deserve to be loved'. You may feel that you're being pulled apart.

Sometimes you may find yourself behaving in ways that seem strange and out of character. You may think, 'I don't know why I did it; it's not really me'. Maybe you really want a loving, supportive relationship, but you unconsciously behave in ways that aren't compatible with achieving this goal. Your behaviour may sabotage the goal even though that wasn't your intention. Your emotions may be inconsistent. One minute you feel happy and the next you feel sad without knowing why. You may talk about having 'part-time problems'. You may say things like, 'I never have enough security in my relationships', but if someone asks you, 'Are you sure?' you'll say, 'No. Sometimes I think I have, and sometimes I think I haven't'. If you experience conflicting feelings or act in inconsistent ways it's a sure indication that you have what's termed a 'parts conflict'.

Don't worry. Fortunately, you can resolve this inner conflict easily by doing 'The Becoming Whole' process that follows. Simply read the instructions through once and follow the steps.

The Becoming Whole Spell

Step 1. Cast your mind back to the relationships you've had. Do you notice recurring problems? How were you feeling? How were you behaving? What do you feel conflicted about? How is that a problem? How exactly is your inner conflict a problem for you? Explain how the conflict has influenced your behaviour. Here are some examples of conflicts and problems identified by my former clients. One woman commented, 'A part of me sabotages everything I do'. A young man said, 'A part of me doesn't think I deserve to be happy'. Another woman felt that a part of her wanted her to feel bad. These clients have identified very obvious problem parts in their unconscious minds.

We'd all have a problem if a part of us sabotages everything we do or if a part of us doesn't think we deserve to be happy. We end up being influenced by the problem part and often behaving (unconsciously) in ways that create unhappy situations for ourselves. Once you find your real conflict or problem part of you, proceed to step 2.

Step 2. Place your arms out in front of you with your palms upturned. Have your elbows slightly out from your body, and *don't* rest your arms on the arms of a chair. Your arms need to be able to move freely. Close your eyes and go inside your unconscious mind. Now address yourself to that part of your unconscious mind that is the problem. Many people find that the problem part often takes the form of a person. So you can ask the part whether it would like to come out and stand on one hand. Now, ask the opposite part, the flip side of the problem part, the positive part, to come out and stand on the opposite hand.

Step 3. Does the problem part look like anyone you recognise? Does it sound like someone you know or feel like someone you're familiar with? Does it remind you of anyone? How about its opposite number? Does it look or sound like anyone you recognise?

Step 4. Start with the problem part and ask what the purpose of the behaviour is. For example, if the problem part was 'sabotaging your relationships', you would ask 'What is the purpose of sabotaging my relationships?' Then you would use the following questions with each answer that comes up.

What is the purpose of_____? If the answer is X?
What is the intention of ____X____? If the answer is Y?
What does _____Y_____ do for you? If the answer is Z?
What is purpose of _____Z_____? And so on.

For example, my client had a problem part of her unconscious mind that was sabotaging everything she did, so I began by asking 'What is the purpose of sabotaging everything you do?' She responded, 'To make me feel bad'. I asked, 'What does that do for you?' She replied, 'To keeping me down'. I then asked, 'What's the purpose in keep you down?' She replied, 'To make me feel safe'. I further inquired, 'And what does feeling safe do for you?' She answered, 'It makes me feel loved'. I said, 'So the intention of the behaviour of this problem part (sabotaging everything you do) is actually to make you feel loved?'

We can see a clear contradiction here between the behaviour and its highest intention. The problem part will then dissolve because we have exposed this contradiction.

As you go through this questioning process, you'll know that you have discovered what the part really wants for you because the answer will be a good thing and a revelation to you. You'll also notice that your hands will begin to come together. You must keep asking the questions until you reach this Level and your hands come together without your conscious effort.

Step 5. Go to the other part, the positive part on the other hand, and ask the same questions to find its highest intention. You'll find that it will eventually reach the same or a similar highest intention as the problem part.

Step 6. Treat each part with courtesy and respect. Notice that each part has knowledge and wisdom and that each has a highest positive intention for you. Notice what both parts agree on and that both parts have been valuable. Ask each part if it's aware that it was once part of a larger whole. Also ask both parts if they would like to become whole again. Finally, ask if any other parts would like to join the integration. Your hands will come together and the two parts will merge into one. Allow your cupped hands to come in towards your heart as you merge the parts into a whole.

Step 7. Carefully consider the following questions: What difference has this exercise made? How do you feel? What will be different the next time you face a situation in which you felt conflict before?

Free Yourself From the Past – Cut the Connecting Cords

Some of us find it difficult to move on and form a new relationship because we are holding on to a past relationship which we know is over, or to someone we need to move on from. Fortunately, there is a wonderful technique from the ancient healing system of Huna which can help us let go of the past and free us to move ahead in our lives.

According to this healing system, we all have an energy field that surround us. When we meet another person we connect our energy. This means that all of us are connected by cords of energy, and energy flows back and forth through these cords. You are connected by this subtle energy to everyone who has ever been in your life.

At certain times in your life you will need to cut a connecting cord if it has become unhealthy and clogged with emotional 'stuff', or when you just need to be free from the energy of another person. This doesn't necessarily mean that you must permanently sever all contact, but you may choose to do just that. Cutting the cord means that you get rid of all the emotional baggage and rubbish in the connection. You can, if you want to, re-establish a cleaner connection later. You may of course choose to never reconnect with the person, and let them go on in their life in whatever way they are meant to, in order that they too grow and learn.

So, if you would like to cut the energy cord with any person (past or present) here's what I'd like you to do.

1.   Think of the connection you have with the person and think of a memory that reminds you of this connection. Now create a stage above the old memory.
2.   Invite the person up onto the stage. See the person as they are in front of you and notice the energy cord connecting you. Can you see or feel or sense the connecting cord?

3. Now visualise an infinite source of healing light and energy floating above your head. Feel it flowing down through the top of your head, filling your whole body with light and warmth. Feel it filling you up so much that it flows out of your heart and down through the cord, healing the person on stage. Gently ask the other person if you have their permission to send them light and healing.

4. Now talk with the other person. Explain clearly what impact their actions have had on your life. Help them to understand what took place with you. Let them know you are telling them this to help them grow and learn from the experience. Then listen carefully to what they have to say.

5. The most important part of cutting the cord is forgiveness. You can let go of a troubling emotion, and get on with your life, when you forgive. So talk about forgiveness in a way that is best for both of you and which helps you both grow and learn. Say what you need to say in order let go of all the negative emotions you hold in relation to this person.

6. Now tell this person you are going to cut the cord and let them go on their own journey to the light and that they will merge with the light and become whole and healed. You will need to let them know if the disconnection is permanent or to establish a cleaner connection. If it is permanent, assure them that moving on is in their best interest and it will allow them to reach their full potential and purpose in life.

7. Imagine you have a large pair of scissors, and cut the cord right up against your skin. Pull the cord inside and put a cap on the end, and heal the hole over where it once was. Note: it is very important you do it this way. If you cut the cord halfway between you and the other person, you are still taking in the 'stuff' through the remainder of the cord you take inside. By cutting the cord right next to your skin, you avoid taking in their 'stuff'. Similarly, by putting a cap on the end of the cord, you are stopping it from going out and finding someone similar to attach it to. So make sure you've pulled it in, capped it and healed the hole.

8. See the other end of the cord go back into the person's body.

See them float up above the stage and move upwards towards the light. Watch as they become smaller and smaller until they are only a dot against the light of the sun. Know that they have become whole and part of the healing light and energy of the sun. 9. Now see the younger you in that old memory. How is that younger you doing now that you have cut the cord? How is the event now that the cord is cut? Knowing what you now know, it makes no sense to hold on to old troubling emotions. Let them go now, and go on with your life in peace.

The Crystal Spell - Seeing Relationships from a New Perspective

The final technique in this Level helps you to see events and people in a better light. It helps you to understand yourself and your relationships more clearly. The crystal spell is more commonly known as 'perceptual positions' in psychology circles. In Level 4, 'Making a Connection – Going Beyond Attraction', you learned that the secret of getting on well with another person is to see things through that person's eyes. The crystal spell helps you to understand why the person behaves in a particular way. Often people behave the way they do to achieve some purpose or fulfil some need. Most people have positive intentions, even when their behaviour appears hurtful or contrary to your needs and interests. Seeing things from the other person's viewpoint changes your beliefs about any given situation and behaviour.

If you're currently experiencing conflict in any relationship, put the crystal spell to the test. You can use this exercise to deal with any relationship, whether it's with a prospective partner, a co-worker, a family member or a friend. Any time you don't seem to be communicating effectively or the dynamic of the relationship is strained, or you feel angry or upset by the other person, this technique will help you understand the relationship, learn from it and learn more about the other person. This knowledge will help you to resolve the conflict and move forward.

The Crystal Spell - Seeing Relationships from a New Perspective

1. The first step in this process is to identify the problem scenario or relationship. Adopt what's called first position. That is, you're looking at the situation from your own perspective. Go back to that time. Look out at the person or person(s) you had the problem with. See what you saw, hear what you heard, feel what you felt. What were you saying? What were they saying? In this position ask yourself the following questions:
   a. How am I behaving?
   b. How am I feeling?
   c. What do I believe about this situation?
   d. What's important to me about this situation?
   e. What can I learn from this situation?

2. Move into second position. That is, you're looking at the situation from the other person's viewpoint. So imagine floating out the top of your head and into the other person, looking back at yourself. Now ask the following questions, answering as the person you have the conflict with:
   a. How are you behaving?
   b. How are you feeling?
   c. What do you believe about this situation?
   d. What's important to you about this situation?
   e. What can you learn from this position?
   f. How has your perception changed?

3. Move into third position, which is a neutral observer position. Imagine floating out the top of the other person's head and becoming an observer who can see both you and the other person. Then answer the following questions as the observer:
   a. How is each of them behaving?
   b. How is each of them feeling?
   c. What beliefs does each appear to be acting on?
   d. What's important to each of them about this situation?

e. What can each of them learn from this position?

f. How has their perception changed?

4. Finally, float up out of the observer back down through the top of your head into yourself, looking through your own eyes. Be aware of all that you've learned from the different perspectives you've experienced. Decide on the best course of action to resolve this problem.

When you take second position you're trying to understand the person from his or her viewpoint. By doing so you may realise that if you had experienced what that person experienced, if you knew what they knew, and if you wanted what they wanted, you might well act the way they're acting even though from your own perspective their behaviour may seem hurtful or uncaring. Seeing from the other person's perspective doesn't justify that person's behaviour, but it does help you understand it and possibly influence it.

Healing the Past and Looking Forward to the Future

By healing your past you will feel much more secure and relaxed in your relationship in the future. The bonds between you and your future partner will be stronger because you are emotionally stronger and at peace with yourself. If you've had troubling experiences in the past, it may be worth investing in the services of a counsellor to work these issues through. It will be well worth the investment. It can be tempting to lean on your partner and rely on them for reassurance and support, but the stronger you are emotionally, the stronger and more equal your relationship will be.

Sometimes my clients say they are worried their old negative feelings will come back or that their new found confidence will not last. What is important to understand is that self-confidence and self-esteem are in-built in all humans, we were born with confidence. To illustrate this universal, natural, inherent self-confidence we all have, let's take as an example a baby learning

148

to walk. Babies learn to walk at a very early stage, before they can talk or understand what is being said to them. As they learn, they'll fall over and pick themselves up time and time again. Although they fall over literally hundreds of times, they keep on trying. The reason they keep going is because this tenacity and confidence (that they will walk) isn't learned or engendered by parents' and relatives' encouragement - it is innate. They instinctively know that sooner or later they will do it (and of course they do).

However, due to circumstances in our lives, many of us lose touch with our natural belief in ourselves and come to distrust and criticise ourselves. This undermines our natural confidence. We can therefore unlearn our tendency to worry, criticise and distrust ourselves. Our job is to rid ourselves of the 'muck' (negative emotions and unproductive beliefs) we have accumulated over our lives and bring to the fore our cleaner, healthier, natural self who has all the self-confidence we need.

Your task is to learn to trust and accept yourself again, and when you do you will recognise your true power. When you trust and value yourself:

- You know who you are, and what you will and will not accept.
- You know what your rhythm of life is, and you move by it.
- You are able to make a decision without arguing with yourself afterward, and without being talked out of how you feel.
- You have self-control, because you understand that the only true power you have is control over yourself.

So suppose that you've healed your emotions so that they can no longer hinder or harm you. Suppose that you've resolved any conflicts you may have had in your present and past relationships. Suppose that any limiting decisions you made about relationships have disappeared, and you no longer hold any self-limiting beliefs. How much happier do you feel? How much freer? How much more motivated are you about achieving what you want in a relationship? How much more do you expect from a relationship?

In the final Level you'll learn how to program your future to get exactly the kind of relationship you've always wanted.

Your Practical Magic for Level 7

1.   Use the 'Lynch Pin' questionnaire to discover the root cause of what is holding you back from having the relationship you truly desire.

2.   Use 'Problem banisher' to release this problem pattern.

3.   Use 'the becoming whole' process when you are aware of any inner conflicts or when you know that your behaviour is incompatible with what you want.

4.   Pick a relationship or scenario that has been causing you trouble. Then view it through the 'crystal' to give you a new understanding of the situation and the person.

You have come a long, long way. You now understand yourself and your past relationships far better. You are now ready to cast a spell over your future to make it exactly the way you want it. You are ready to proceed to the final Level.

Conclusion

The Higher Plane – Your Future Happiness

You've reached the final stage, and you stand at the beginning of your journey into your future. You've come a long way. You know what it takes to change your life and create the life you want to live. You know that happiness is a choice. You know exactly what you want from a relationship and the quickest and easiest way to get it.

You understand what drives you and what you value most in a relationship and in your life. You know what your purpose in life is. You know how to set goals for your life and your relationship so that you can make them happen. You know the essence of what you want. You know how to create emotional freedom for yourself. You know how to generate fantastic feelings whenever you want them, in any situation. You can now build relationships more easily. You know how to attract people, and you know the secret of charisma. You can boost your self-confidence easily whenever you need to. You've released any harmful emotions from your past, and you've resolved any internal conflicts you may have had. You've also released any unconscious decisions and beliefs that were holding you back. Now you have the power to create the life and love you want.

Abraham Lincoln once said: 'Most people are about as happy as they make up their minds to be'.

The most important thing to remember is that happiness, just like any other emotion, is first and foremost a choice. You now have that choice. Never forget it and if you are wise you will exercise your power for the rest of your life. Yes, indeed. You've come a very long way. Well done.

The Spell for an Amazingly Happy Future!

Now it's time to look to your future and to create it exactly the way you want it. The first step to creating the future you want is to set a SMART goal (as you did in Level 2), and then insert your goal into your future using 'The River of your Future' spell. The second step is to practice a simple, pleasant daily programming routine that helps you to focus consistently on what you want.

By inserting a goal in your future and consistently focusing on what you want, your unconscious mind will naturally and continually work towards achieving your dreams, whether you're consciously aware of it or not. Provided that your love goal is SMART (see Level 2) and that it fits in with your purpose in life, you can take action consciously and unconsciously to achieve what you most desire in life. With your conscious and unconscious mind working together to move you towards your goal, you're ten times more likely to achieve what you want. You can help yourself to create your future exactly the way you want it by inserting all of your goals into the river of your life. Here's how.

Making the Goal SMART

First, make sure your goal is SMART. Review the procedure outlined in Level 2:

S: Specific/Simple. The goal must be clear, simple and unambiguous.

M: Measurable/Meaningful. You must be able to measure the goal. It must be meaningful to you, instigated by you and for you.

A: 'As if now'/Achievable. Express your goal as if you already have it. Goals must be stated in the present tense, for example, 'I'm involved in a loving, committed relationship'. 'Act as if' you've already achieved your goal.

R: Realistic/Responsible. You must be one hundred percent sure that this goal can be achieved. The goal must also be responsible. Achieving it must not harm you or any other person.

T: Timed towards what you want. You should have a precise day, month and year by which you want to achieve your goal. Setting a specific deadline gives your unconscious mind precise instructions about when you want your goal, and it will work towards achieving it at that exact time.

To make sure your goal is SMART, use the 'Keys to Achieving Your Goals' in Level 2. Once you have a clear, achievable goal, follow these steps to insert it into the river of your future and enchant your future to be exactly the way you want it.

The River of Time Spell - Your Relationship Goal in Your Future

1. Figure out the last step. What's absolutely the last thing that must happen so that you know you've reached your goal? For example, you are hand in hand with your spouse looking out over your garden. Or you're dancing in each other's arms at your wedding reception. Or you are enjoying a wonderful walk in the forest. Imagine you have achieved your love goal.
2. As you think of this last thing, see what you see, feel what you feel, hear what you hear.
3. Make sure you're in your body, looking through your own eyes. Really feel those amazing feelings. Make the picture brighter and bigger. Adjust it in any way necessary to make the feeling even more intense.
4. When it's intense and you're feeling wonderful, step out of the picture and see yourself in it.
5. In your mind's eye, take this picture or internal representation and float up out of your body. Float as high as possible into the air. Look down and see yourself far below sitting on a riverbank. Imagine a beautiful silvery river extending in both directions. The river is your life. Look out toward the future along the river as it goes into the distance.
6. Bring your internal representation to life with four deep breaths. Breathe in deeply, right to the bottom of your lungs,

filling them up to the top. Then blow all that energy into your internal representation.

7. Taking the internal representation with you, float above your river of life out into the future.

8. At the appropriate place where it feels right to you, drop your internal representation down into your river of life, then let go. Let it float right down into your future. See, feel and hear it merge into your future.

9. Watch the events between then and now re-evaluate themselves to support your goal.

10. Float back to now.

11. 'Act as if' you've already achieved your goal. If you knew for certain that the loving relationship you really desire is in your future, that it was a foregone conclusion, how would you behave differently now?

Once you put a goal in your future you can forget about it. Your unconscious mind will work towards achieving it for you. Knowing that you'll achieve your love goal, you can relax and really enjoy your life. You can actively and creatively go about building the life you want. What you've done in the past has created your present, and what you do now is creating your future. Only you can make your future fantastic, just the way you want it.

Finally, to stay on track, reinforce your success. You can keep focused using the Daily Positive Enchantment Routine. It's specifically aimed at enabling you to find and maintain the relationship of your dreams. I use this routine every morning to set myself up for a great day. By taking this little time to divine your mind with positive images and suggestions, you'll have more energy, you'll feel more motivated and you'll become happier and more confident as you achieve your relationship goals.

Your Daily Positive Enchantment Routine

1. Begin by taking a deep breath. As you breathe out, feel

relaxation spread from your feet up your calves and shins, over your knees and deep into your thighs. Count one. Breathe in deeply again. As you breathe out, feel the warm relaxation flow up from your thighs into your pelvis and hips, through your abdomen and up to your waist. Count two. Breathe in again. As you breathe out, feel relaxation spread through your chest and ribs, up and over your shoulders and down your arms to the fingertips. Count three. Take another deep breath. As you breathe out, allow the relaxing feeling to flow up your neck into your head and feel all your facial muscles relaxing. Count four. Breathe in again, and then breathe out from the top of your head down, allowing your whole body to relax as you breathe out slowly. Relax.

2.   Imagine the qualities of your authentic self. See how you look as your authentic self, feel how you feel. Step into your authentic self and see yourself going through your day.

3.   Go back to a time when you felt really, really happy. I mean ecstatic! Float into your body. See what you saw, hear what you heard, really feel those feelings of pure ecstasy. Double the feeling. Treble it. Let the feelings become as intense as possible.

4.   Next, go back to a time when you felt truly loved, not necessarily by a partner. You may have a beautiful memory of feeling loved by a friend, a parent, a pet, or you may recall a spiritual or religious experience. Whatever your experience of feeling loved or cared about, go back to that time. Float into your body, see what you saw, and hear what you heard, really feel those feelings of love and care. Double the feeling. Treble it!

5.   Sit up straight, shoulders down and relaxed. Take a deep breath. Think about feeling powerful and strong, and go back to a time when you actually felt totally powerful and confident. Float into your body, see what you saw, and hear what you heard, feel the power and confidence. Double the feeling. Treble it! Notice how great you feel.

6.   Bring to mind your internal representation of having achieved your relationship goal. That is, visualise yourself having achieved your goal. See yourself in your picture. How do you look? How

do you sound? How do you feel? Make the picture brighter and bolder. Know that achieving your goal is a foregone conclusion. Really enjoy it. Feel how good it feels.

7. Take a deep breath through your nose and breathe out with your mouth gently open, making a 'haa' sound. Let each inhalation fill you with energy and let each exhalation energise all your goals.

As you get used to the routine you'll be able to complete it in as little as ten minutes. However, I recommend that, whenever possible, you take at least fifteen minutes to set yourself up for a wonderful day.

The Spell for Releasing the Goddess

So you are now one of the lucky ones who know how to be successful in love. You have the power to create the kind of love life you want and be the kind of lover you want to be. To help release your (sex) goddess, I have one final luxurious technique.

Meet Your Venus

1. Close your eyes. Take three deep breathes. Feel your body relax.
2. Imagine a wonderful exotic location. A beautiful tropical beach fringed with palm trees, or a luxurious spa, or historic little Italian village. Whatever feels great to you.
3. See yourself in this place, looking fantastic and feeling sensual and relaxed.
4. Visualise yourself looking confident, attractive and sexy. Notice what you are wearing. Notice your stance, pose and elegance. See an inner radiance shining through.
5. Watch yourself talking with others. See how they react to you. Notice their admiring glances.
6. Now step into your body and look out through your own eyes. Know what it feels like to look this great, sexy and beautiful.

You have met your goddess and she is fantastic, isn't she?

Really feel what it's like to be her. Feel her sensuality, confidence, passion, poise, contentment and eroticism. This is a woman who knows what she wants in love and will have it. This is a woman who is happy and comfortable in herself. Whenever you're going out, just step into this wonderful sensuous creature and enjoy being desired!

Charismatic people are charismatic because they feel comfortable in their own skins. They are relaxed and content with who they are, they are not looking for the approval of others as this doesn't concern them too much. Neither are they trying to manipulate others into liking them. It is precisely because of this relaxed, carefree air they exude that we are drawn to them.

Valuing and respecting yourself means that you will do things at your own pace. You will take your time and get to know individuals you are dating. Only when you are ready and as sure as you can be about a man's feelings and intentions will you sleep with him. Valuing yourself means you are confident in making a man wait to sleep with you. If he truly desires you he will wait and he will consider himself lucky to wait. If he has to wait to sleep with you, he'll not only see you as more beautiful, he'll also take the time to appreciate who you are. So take your time to tune into your feelings and observe how he behaves towards you.

Sherry Argove lets us into a secret that men don't want women to know. When a man meets a woman, he almost immediately puts her into one of two categories: 'good time only' or 'worthwhile'. Watch out! Because the second he pops you into that 'good time only' category, you almost never come back out. So don't be in any hurry. Give yourself some time and ask yourself, 'Does he make me feel valued, desired and appreciated? Is he willing to take the time to get to know me?'

If the relationship and the man are right for you, it will feel easy and effortless. You'll feel relaxed and happy when he does call, and relaxed and confident when he doesn't. If you feel you are jumping through hoops, working hard and worrying when he doesn't call, then it may not be the right relationship for you. As in any other area of your life, you know you are on the right track when you feel happy and good about yourself.

How Great Will Your Life Be from Now On? Recognise Your Power

We're now reaching the end of the book and you're thinking about your future. You'll recall that I began this journey with you by commenting that people who have happy, loving, committed long-term relationships aren't simply lucky; rather, they've created this happiness for themselves by acting, thinking, and feeling in certain ways. You now have the information, knowledge, skills and beliefs to do the same for yourself. It really is about loving yourself, truly loving yourself, and feeling that you deserve good things and happiness.

As you move forward, fill your mind and body with the life-affirming notion that you deserve the very best and you are prepared to do what it takes to get it. This time you are not prepared to settle for less. You *can* feel safe and secure, and at the same time free to be who you really are when you are in love. In fact, you understand, if you don't feel like this then it's not love. By working on yourself, you have changed your deep-seated beliefs about the love that you deserve. Because of this, you exude self-confidence and are beginning to attract the very love you want.

Because men are good at hiding their feelings, woman are often unsure of whether a man is in love with her or simply enjoying her company until something better comes along. The important point is, if you are debating with yourself about whether he loves you or not, and you've been together for some time, you might be settling for less. You know in your heart of hearts whether he loves you. All you need to do is close your eyes, focus within, and ask yourself, 'Does he love me?' Your body will tell you the answer. You don't have to ask him, he doesn't have to tell you, you will just know.

As you accept, love and respect yourself, so you can love and respect others. You become a magnet that draws love and harmony into your life. It is important that you are aware of this, so notice the little acts of love and kindness that are all around you, that you may not have noticed before. The law of attraction tells us that what you give out, you will attract back to you. Because of this, be absolutely confident that you will create the loving relationship you desire. When you do, invest in this relationship in the way you are investing in yourself. Give kindness, acceptance and respect to yourself and your partner.

When the person you desire feels that you really understand and accept them, they will not be able to resist you. No amount of rationalisation or logic will be able to stop them from falling in love with you. Their ability to resist loving you will go out the window.

Talk to one another and recognise that you are different and have different ways of showing and receiving love. Find out what makes your partner feel loved, and let him know what makes you feel cherished and appreciated. If you consciously invest in creating the loving relationship you want, you'll enjoy the benefits in years to come.

Respect your partner for who they are, in the same way that you would want and expect them to respect you. Consciously investing and nurturing a loving relationship will bring you support, commitment, love and joy. Your investment will continue to pay you dividends in years to come. One of the ways you can do this is through expressing your love for each other in as many ways as you can. Each of us has our own different ways of giving and receiving love, and many of us fall into the trap of thinking we know what our partner wants and needs. Don't make any assumptions here or think you can read your partner's mind. Tell your partner what you would like and don't forget to ask the same from him. What makes you feel loved and appreciated? Does he need to tell you something or speak to you in a certain way, do you need him to touch you and hold you, or do you need him to give you some other form of demonstration of his love for you? What makes your partner feel loved? Are you sure you know?

For any relationship to work really well, you must focus on what you love and appreciate about the other person, and not on what you don't like. When you focus on their strengths and good qualities, you'll see more of them and you'll get more of them.

You are demonstrating to your partner that you value them for who they truly are. This is the most wonderful precious gift that you can give to anyone. Their response to the gift will tell you if this is the wonderful, loving, supportive relationship that you deserve.

After all is said and done, the one question that is always present for both of you in a relationship is, 'How important and how valuable am I to you really?' All other questions are merely tangents of this one. The more valued and important each of you feels to the other, the stronger and warmer will be you and your partner's feelings of love in return.

It is often said that it is the little things that matter so much, and this is doubly so in a loving relationship. It is easy and it costs nothing to sincerely compliment your partner and give them warm words of encouragement. It's important to tell your partner what you like about them. By genuinely praising, supporting and encouraging them, you build trust and respect. So help to boost their self-esteem by adding the odd genuine compliment.

As time goes by, if you nurture acceptance, trust and respect in your relationship, you will notice the loving bond between you grow stronger.

The more time a relationship between two people has to grow and mature, the stronger the bonds of emotional attachment will be. Happy and successful relationships are based on understanding – of yourself, your partner and how you relate. It is also important to remember that as time goes by you and your partner will change. This is only natural and these changes can keep a relationship alive and interesting. Our circumstances can change too and this may not always be in ways that we want. Sometimes change can be painful. We may be attached to the way things were. We may have to adjust to a new way of thinking or a new way of life. It may also mean letting go of things that have been familiar and safe.

You'll need to be flexible to adapt. Look for the opportunities that change can provide. See changes as opportunities for new growth and deeper intimacy. In healthy, successful relationships, individuals learn to adapt and change together. They accept that change is a natural part of life and being human, and they support each other through all their life changes.

A New Wave of Positive Change

The world we live in has changed in astonishing ways in a remarkably short time. You and I have seen amazing technological changes in our lifetime, particularly in the means of communication, as did our parents and grandparents. At one time people contacted each other by letter if they lived some distance apart. Often letters took days or even weeks to arrive. Then the telegraph made it possible for messages to arrive quickly over huge distances. Then came the telephone, followed by radio, television, fax, and video, DVD, the Internet, e-mail and mobile phones. The creative technology of communication is constantly being upgraded and renewed. By logging on to the Internet we can communicate with each other across the earth in an instant. All this new technology means more information to absorb, more to learn and more opportunities than ever before.

Every day, more people are recognising that the mind is a powerful magical creative force that they have not yet utilised to its full potential to create the lives that they want. A growing body of scientists is convinced of the power of thought, not only to heal, but also to affect our DNA and even the molecular structure of substances like water. We stand at the beginning of a profound change in ideas about what causes transformation - of our own lives and of the world around us.

One could argue that nowadays a country's real wealth is not gauged by material resources, but by the ideas and innovations of individuals, their practical application and ability to create wealth. The real source of wealth is our minds, and those people with the brightest ideas, the ideas that bring true value to people's lives will create the greatest wealth in the world. Every single one of us is lucky to own one of the most valuable, powerful and magical gifts in the world. It is free and it is here right between our ears!

To be part of this new wave of change you need to direct your attention inwards. What you're thinking and believing now is creating the life you'll live in the future. The life that you're now leading is the result of your thoughts in the past. What can you do to change your thinking and beliefs to change your life and your relationships, to make them exactly the way you want them? It's up to you. You are in charge of your life and your feelings.

Your partner can be wonderful for you. He can encourage you, support you and advise you. But understand, that is all he can do, he cannot make you feel happy, or make you feel calm in a crisis, or make everything all right for you. A loving, committed relationship will provide the supportive context where both partners can grow and develop emotionally and spiritually.

The poet Kahlil Gibran expresses this sentiment wonderfully in his beautiful poem 'The Prophet':

And stand together, yet not too near together:
For the pillars of the temple stand apart
And the oak tree and the cypress grow
not in each other's shadow.

Through your relationship with your partner you learn about yourself. It is a mirror reflecting what is going on inside you. In any relationship, ask yourself, 'What is this telling me about myself? Who am I really?' Remember you are in charge of your learning, your growth and your spiritual evolution. You are always in charge of you.

It is argued that a new age of psycho-technology is upon us. The widespread application of NLP, Thought Field Therapy, Emotional Freedom Technique and other psychological tools of self-empowerment are testimony of this. Their use in this book is part of this new age of magical psycho-technology, and they will help you to change your life and your relationships for the better.

Your mind is a valuable and powerful piece of technology, and your thoughts and ideas can create love and abundance. Focus on bringing love into your life and it will come.

We now know that love is the most powerful and the highest frequency of all, and that happiness, joy and all good feelings are on the frequency of love. Your have the ability to generate unlimited feelings of love. You are in harmony with the universe when you can feel and express feelings of love. Look for love all around you, see it everywhere. Look for opportunities to love things and people. Focus on things you love, the activities you enjoy doing, the things that make you feel good, the situations in which you are happiest. If you look for, and feel, joy and love, you will feel that love and happiness returning to you ten times over. The universe will send you even more things to love and enjoy. It will seem as though there is a force that is doing everything for you, bringing every good thing and positive person into your life.

You've learned some amazing ways to get your unconscious mind to work for you. The techniques that you've practiced will begin to bring about more benefits each day. It's great that you've chosen to invest time and energy into creating the relationship you desire and deserve. This decision will enhance the quality of your life many times over.

You have the responsibility to practice the techniques in this book and to guide your mind to achieving what you most want in life. As you achieve success in your relationships, you'll be part of a small group of people who are consciously utilising the whole power of their minds to create the type of world they want. You're becoming a trailblazer. Others will want to learn from you. You'll be one of the 'lucky' people with wonderful relationships and a wonderful life that you've really created for yourself.

As you go on to achieve the relationship of your dreams, I'll say 'Namaste' and leave you to dwell on this traditional greeting in India:

Namaste
I honour the place in you where the entire universe dwells.
I Honour the place in you of love, light and peace.
When you're in that place in you, and I'm in that place in me,
we are one.
Until we meet again,
Joanne Coyle

Acknowledgments

I am indebted to Richard Bandler and John Grinder the originators of Neuro-Linguistic Programming.

References for Level 6

Gross, J., 'Emotional Expression in Cancer Onset and Progression'. *Social Science and Medicine*, 1989 28, (12), 1239-48.

Hamilton, David, R., *It's the Thought that Counts.* Bonnybridge: Hamilton, 2005.

Loehr, James, *Stress for Success.* City:Three Rivers Press, 1998.

Miller, Carolyn, *Creating Miracles.* CA: Kramer Inc.

Pennebaker, J. W., Kiecolt-Glaser, J.K. and Glaser. R., 'Disclosure of Traumas and Immune Function: Health Implications for Psychotherapy', *Journal of Consult. Clinical Psychology* (56) 1988, 239–45.

Rein, G., Atkinson, M. and McCarty, R., 'The Physiological and Psychological Effects of Compassion and Anger'. *Journal of Advancement in Medicine*, 1995, 8 (2), 87–105.

Spiegel, D., Bloom, J. and Kramer, H. C., 'Effect of Psychological Treatment on Survival of Patients with Metastatic Breast Cancer'. *Lancet*, 1989, 2, 888–91.

Bibliography and Recommended Reading

Argove, Sherry, *Why Men Love Goddesses.* Avon, Massachusetts: Adams Media Corporation, 2002.

Bandler, Richard, and Grinder, John, *The Structure of Magic 1.* City: Science and Behaviour Books, 1975.

Field, Lynda, *Weekend Love Coach: How to get the love you want in 48 hours.* London: Vermillion, 2005.

Gibran, Kahlil, *The Prophet.* London: Heinemann, 1926.

Gee, Ariana, and Gregory, Mary, *Be Your Own Love Coach.* London: New Holland, 2005.

Grinder, John, and Bandler, Richard,*The Structure of Magic 2.* Science and Behaviour Books, 1975.

Hamilton, David, R., *It's the Thought that Counts.* Bonnybridge: Hamilton, 2005.

Hamilton, David, R., *Destiny vs. Freewill*, London: Hay House,

2007.

McKnight, Thomas, and Phillips, Robert, H., *Love Tactics: How to Win the One You Want*. New York: Square One, 2002.

O'Connor, Joseph, *The NLP Workbook*: A Practical Guide to Achieving the Results You Want, London: Element, 2003.

Useful Websites

Divine Aspirations: www.divine-aspirations.co.uk (my own website)

Steven Wright, Relationships, Loving is Nothing without Truth, www.healthyplace.net

Some Other Titles From Mirage Publishing

Burnt: One Man's Inspiring Story of Survival - Ian Colquhoun
Cosmic Ordering Guide - Stephen Richards
Cosmic Ordering Connection - Stephen Richards
Cosmic Ordering: Chakra Clearing - Stephen Richards
Cosmic Ordering: Oracle Healing Cards – Stephen Richards
Cosmic Ordering: Oracle Wish Cards – Stephen Richards & Karen Whitelaw Smith
Mrs Darley's Pagan Whispers: A Celebration of Pagan Festivals, Sacred Days, Spirituality and Traditions of the Year – Carole Carlton
Past Life Tourism - Barbara Ford-Hammond
The Butterfly Experience: Inspiration For Change - Karen Whitelaw Smith
The Hell of Allegiance: My Living Nightmare of being Gang Raped and Held for Ten days by the British Army – Charmaine Maeer with Stephen Richards
The Real Office: An Uncharacteristic Gesture of Magnanimity by Management Supremo Hilary Wilson-Savage - Hilary Wilson-Savage
The Tumbler: Kassa (Košice) – Auschwitz – Sweden - Israel - Azriel Feuerstein

Fothcoming titles
Life Without Lottie - Fiona Fridd
Psychic Salon - Barbara Ford-Hammond
Rebel Diet: They Don't Want You To Have It! – Emma James

Mirage Publishing Website:
www.miragepublishing.com

Submissions of Mind, Body & Spirit manuscripts
welcomed from new authors.